LOST RAILW
OF
THE CHILTERNS

Leslie Oppitz

COUNTRYSIDE BOOKS

NEWBURY, BERKSHIRE

COUNTRYSIDE BOOKS
3 Catherine Road
Newbury, Berkshire

To view our complete range of books,
please visit us at
www.countrysidebooks.co.uk

ISBN 1 85306 643 5

The cover picture shows LMS 'Black 5' locomotive 5379
hauling a passenger set southwards under the bridge at Wendover
on the former Metropolitan and Great Central Railway
(From an original painting by Colin Doggett)

Produced through MRM Associates Ltd., Reading
Typeset by Techniset Typesetters, Newton-le-Willows
Printed by Woolnough Bookbinding Ltd., Irthlingborough

CONTENTS

ABBREVIATIONS

The following abbreviations are used in this book:

A&BR	Aylesbury & Buckingham Railway
ASLEF	Associated Society of Locomotive Engineers and Firemen
B&CR	Bedford & Cambridge Railway
BR	British Rail
BTC	British Transport Commission
C&PRR	Chinnor and Princes Risborough Railway
GCR	Great Central Railway
GNR	Great Northern Railway
GW&GC jt	Great Western & Great Central joint
GWR	Great Western Railway
HL&DR	Hertford, Luton & Dunstable Railway
IHPS	Iron Horse Preservation Society
L&BR	London & Birmingham Railway
LBSCR	London, Brighton & South Coast Railway
LCDR	London, Chatham & Dover Railway
LMS	London, Midland & Scottish Railway
LNER	London & North Eastern Railway
LNWR	London & North Western Railway
LPTB	London Passenger Transport Board
M&GC jt	Metropolitan & Great Central joint
MET	Metropolitan Railway
MR	Midland Railway
MS&LR	Manchester, Sheffield & Lincolnshire Railway
O&AT	Oxford & Aylesbury Tramroad
W&PRR	Watlington & Princes Risborough Railway
W&RR	Watford & Rickmansworth Railway
WH&BR	Ware, Hadham & Buntingford Railway

ACKNOWLEDGEMENTS

Acknowledgements go to the numerous libraries and record offices throughout Buckinghamshire, Bedfordshire and Hertfordshire and many of the surrounding areas, where staff have delved into records. Acknowledgements also go to the late J. L. Smith of Lens of Sutton, T. Davey, Barry Hoper, Phil Marsh and John H. Meredith for their help with photographs.

Thanks go to the following who generously contributed with information: Allan Baker, Manager, Sales & Marketing, Buckinghamshire Railway Centre; Peter Harris, Director, Chinnor & Princes Risborough Railway; Edwin Lambert (E & L Film Partnership) of the Leighton Buzzard Narrow Gauge Railway; Ian & Belinda Lodwick of Station House, Westcott; Bill Griffiths, Director, Milton Keynes Museum; Michael Waters, Swanbourne Station House.

Personal thanks go to Brian Butler who produced the maps and especially to my wife, Joan, who toured the Chilterns area with me and who carefully checked the final manuscript.

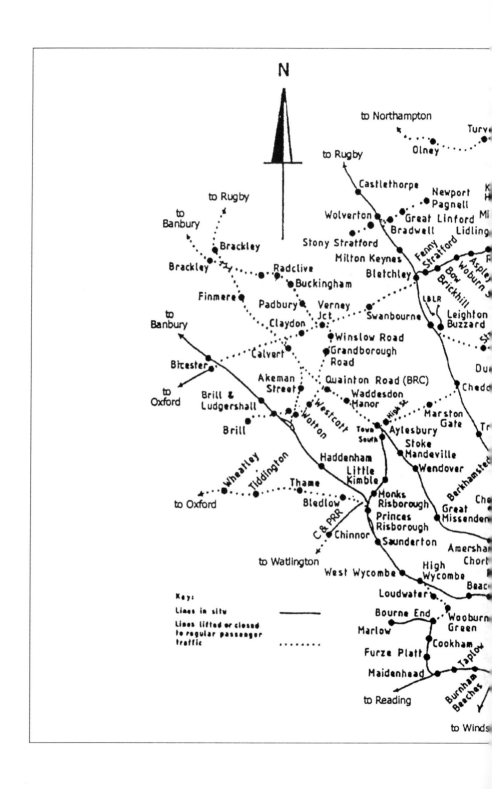

N

to Northampton
Turv
Olney

to Rugby

to Rugby
Castlethorpe
Newport
Pagnell
Wolverton
Great Linford
Stony Stratford
Bradwell
Lidling

to Brackley
Banbury
Brackley
Milton Keynes
Fenny Stratford
Aspley
Woburn S

Brackley
Radclive
Bletchley
Bow
Brickhill

Buckingham

Finmere
Padbury
Verney
Jct
L&LR
Leighton
Buzzard

to Banbury
Claydon
Swanbourne

Winslow Road
Grandborough
Road

Calvert
Bicester

to Oxford
Akeman
Street
Quainton Road (BRC)
Chedd

Brill &
Ludgershall
Waddesdon
Manor
Marston
Gate

Brill
Wotton
Westcott
High St.
Aylesbury
Town
South
Tr

Wheatley
Tiddington
Haddenham
Stoke
Mandeville
Wendover

Thame
Little
Kimble
Berkhamste

to Oxford
Bledlow
Monks
Risborough
Great
Missenden
Che

C & PRR
Chinnor
Princes
Risborough
Amersha
Chort

Saunderton

to Watlington
West Wycombe
High
Wycombe
Beac

Loudwater

Key:
Bourne End
Wooburn
Green

Lines in situ
Marlow
Cookham

Lines lifted or closed
to regular passenger
traffic
Furze Platt
Taplow

Maidenhead
Burnham
Beeches

to Reading

to Winds

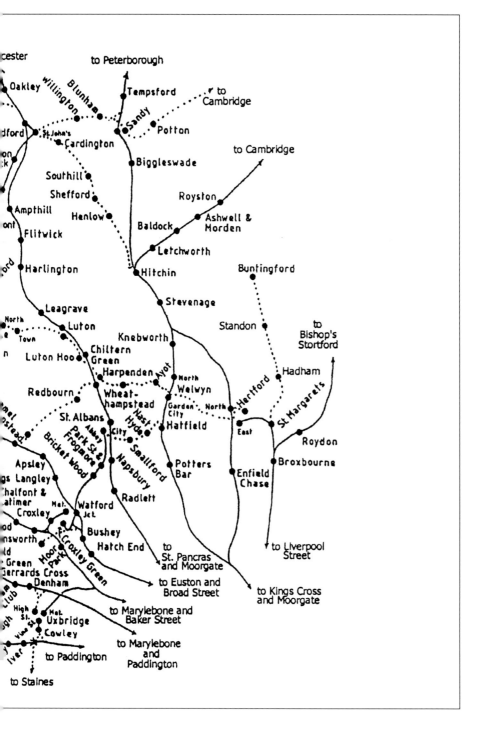

Introduction

Carriage doors slammed, a guard's whistle blew and a steam locomotive edged its way forward as a passenger train slowly moved out of Quainton Road station. The locomotive was GWR 57XX class 0-6-0PT no 7715 (L99). These pannier tanks of the Great Western Railway are probably the best known of all British tank engines. They were first introduced in 1904 as rebuilds of the 2021 class saddletanks, used mainly for freight or light passenger work on the GWR system. The locomotive L99 was hauling three Mk 1 corridor coaches. Yet the train was not bound for Aylesbury or beyond but a run of less than one mile along track owned by the Buckingham Railway Centre. The date was Sunday, 27th June 1999.

A visit to Quainton Road can serve as a fascinating reminder of the many branch lines that once crossed the counties surrounding the Chiltern Hills. Many relics can still be found – old station buildings, engine sheds, road bridges or overgrown trackbeds all go to make up what was once a network of branches throughout the area.

Railways as we know them today evolved in the 1820s from George Stephenson's enthusiasm over locomotive engines. With the opening of the Stockton to Darlington Railway in 1825, the first conventional steam train had arrived. In 1826 a line between Liverpool and Manchester was approved and three years later the famous Rainhill trials took place to establish which type of steam locomotive gave the best means of traction. Travelling was pretty uncomfortable in those early days with railway carriages beginning as stagecoach bodies attached to wagon bases. They were small, cramped and unlit and had no heating or other facilities. When lighting came it was by oil lamps, subsequently to be replaced by gas lamps, and luxuries such as steam heating and comfortable seating came later in the century.

On 1st June 1834, the first major trunk railway to cut through the Chilterns was born when the first sod for the London & Birmingham Railway (L&BR) was cut at Chalk Farm. Work was soon to go ahead and, for three months from 20th July 1837,

Boxmoor (today's Hemel Hempstead) was the railway's temp-orary terminus from the capital while Stephenson pressed northwards. Beyond Tring came the famous Tring Cutting through chalk, 2½ miles long and up to 60 ft deep. To complete the cutting, 1¾ million tons of material had to be removed taking 400 men over three years. On 17th September 1838 Birmingham was reached, providing Midlands industries with access to the markets they sought in London.

By the end of the century, no fewer than five major routes had penetrated the Chilterns. After the L&BR came the Great Northern Railway (GNR), empowered by an Act of June 1846 to build a railway from King's Cross to Doncaster and York. This reached Hitchin in 1850 and was in turn supplemented by the Midland Railway which reached Hitchin from Leicester in 1857. It was not long before the volume of traffic between Hitchin and King's Cross caused considerable congestion and in 1862 the GNR evicted Midland trains from its overcrowded King's Cross sidings. The Midland saw its only future was to build an independent route and this was completed in 1868 between Bedford and St Pancras via Luton and St Albans.

Meantime, in 1854, the Wycombe Railway (with GWR backing) opened a line from Maidenhead to High Wycombe, to be followed in 1862 by an extension from High Wycombe to Thame via Princes Risborough. This became a main route for passengers travelling to London but when the Great Western & Great Central joint line opened in 1906, traffic quickly diverted to Marylebone and Paddington on a shorter and more direct journey.

A fifth route through the Chilterns reached Rickmansworth in 1887 when the Metropolitan Railway built outwards from Baker Street. Chesham was reached in 1889 and Aylesbury in 1892 where it met existing Aylesbury & Buckinghamshire Railway tracks. In 1899 the Great Central Railway (GCR) opened a line between Rugby and Quainton Road as part of a bid by the chairman, Sir Edward Watkin, to link the North and Midlands with London – and eventually beyond to Paris. To reach London they had to use Metropolitan Railway tracks but the ambitious GCR sought an improved route with straighter track and lesser gradients, so a link was opened in 1905 south of Calvert (between Grendon Underwood junction and Ashendon junction) carrying trains across to the Princes Risborough-High Wycombe line.

From these major routes, branch lines developed where steam trains made their way across open stretches of countryside, linking remote villages and towns. In numerous instances passenger traffic remained light throughout, although goods traffic provided an essential service to many agricultural areas. Some lines suffered an early demise simply because they became uneconomic. With road transport fast competing, the Beeching cuts of the early 1960s also took their toll.

This book intends to examine not only the lives of these lines in the counties of Buckinghamshire, Bedfordshire and Hertford-shire, their decline and closure, but also the preserved lines and societies of today that are dedicated to keeping the past alive. It also provides the reader with a means to explore 'lost' stations that can still be found and the numerous trackbeds that have survived, many converted to footpaths.

Leslie Oppitz

1
GWR Lines Westward And A Preserved Railway

Bourne End to High Wycombe
Princes Risborough to Oxford
Princes Risborough to Watlington
The Chinnor & Princes Risborough Railway

GWR Auto-Engine 1442 & W201 awaits departure at Marlow station, 30th July 1949. (John H. Meredith)

Ex-GWR 2-6-2T class 6100 (introduced in 1931 and designed by C. B. Collett) pulls into Wooburn Green station probably early 1950s. (Lens of Sutton)

Bourne End to High Wycombe

The Wycombe Railway was incorporated on 27th July 1846 initially to build a railway from Maidenhead to High Wycombe. This was a single-track broad gauge line, worked from the outset by the GWR. The opening of the line was delayed for a number of years, partly because of financial difficulties and the bankruptcy of its contractor, but despite setbacks services began on 1st August 1854. Maidenhead station is now known as Taplow, and the original intermediate stations were Maidenhead (Wycombe branch), Cookham, Marlow Road (renamed Bourne End in 1874), Wooburn Green (spelt Woburn Green until October 1872) and Loudwater. Maidenhead (Wycombe branch) station, situated close to an overbridge where the Great West Road crossed the track, has today disappeared beyond all trace.

Under an Act of 17th August 1857, the Wycombe Railway obtained powers to extend to Princes Risborough and a later Act

Loudwater station closed to goods traffic in July 1966 and to passengers on 4th May 1970. (Lens of Sutton)

agreed extensions to Oxford and Aylesbury (see chapter 2). With these extensions completed by the mid-1860s, the High Wycombe to Maidenhead branch became the principal route to London for passengers in the High Wycombe and Princes Risborough areas. All Wycombe Railway lines were worked by the GWR and the company's independent existence, owning over 44 miles of broad gauge track, ended on 1st February 1867 when it was absorbed by the GWR. Some three years later the Bourne End to High Wycombe branch was converted to standard gauge track.

The railway reached Marlow in 1873. A short branch from Marlow Road to Marlow was opened on 28th June of that year by the Great Marlow Railway Company. This was also a single line and it was worked by electric train token, being the first GWR branch to use this system. On 1st January 1874 it was decided to change the name of Marlow Road station to Bourne End, thus avoiding any confusion. This short branch was to prosper and the train service became affectionately known as the 'Marlow Donkey'. Like the Wycombe Railway, it was worked by

15

the GWR from the start although it did not amalgamate with the larger company until 1st July 1897.

In 1906 the Great Western & Great Central joint (GW&GC jt) opened a line to London via Beaconsfield which provided a more direct access to the capital, taking just over 6 miles off the earlier route via Bourne End and Maidenhead. Passengers were quick to transfer to the line and the Bourne End branch suffered considerably. Despite this, there were frequent diversions along the branch and larger 4-6-0 and 2-8-0 locomotives could be seen. Trains were normally hauled by GWR class 14XX 0-4-2Ts, some dividing at Bourne End. When the Bourne End to High Wycombe section closed to passengers on 4th May 1970, Bourne End became a junction where Maidenhead trains reversed back to Marlow.

Northwards from Bourne End towards High Wycombe the line continued up the valley of the river Wye, which was once the centre of a paper industry with mill-boards made near Bourne End. At Wooburn Green sidings served paper works. Onward, the line followed the sweep of the Chiltern ridge to Loudwater, the home of Ford's blotting paper. It was from Loudwater that the traveller first caught sight of the GW&GC jt line high up on the adjacent hillside which the branch train would shortly join on its ascent towards High Wycombe. Today part of the line has been consumed by the busy M40 motorway, with its sliproads and roundabouts connecting with the A40.

Princes Risborough to Oxford

Parliament agreed on 28th June 1861 that a line could extend from Princes Risborough to Oxford. Thame was reached on 1st August 1862 although there was no official ceremony. During the afternoon a party of directors and shareholders travelled the line from Wycombe to Thame in three coaches hauled by a 'Sun' class 2-2-2 locomotive named *Sunbeam* with 6 ft diameter driving wheels. A regular service from Paddington to Thame began the following day with four trains each way daily via Maidenhead taking around 2¾ hours. The single fares were 9/-, 6/3d and 4/- for first, second and third class respectively. There was an

16

Wheatley station not long before closure in 1963 looking towards Oxford. In its time the station possessed sidings, a crane and a cattle dock. Unusually there was no footbridge and passengers changing platforms had to use the road bridge. (Lens of Sutton)

intermediate station at Bledlow and a halt at Towersey.

The line was welcomed by the people of Thame, one of its benefits being a reduction in the price of coal. The line was broad gauge, worked by the GWR from the start, and was also the first to use the train staff and ticket system. Work quickly began on the Thame to Oxford section with considerable earthworks required for the construction of Horspath Tunnel nearer the Oxford end of the line. In all, approximately 640,000 cubic yards of blue clay had to be dug out and the tunnel, 1,584 feet in length, had to be lined throughout.

The extension to Kennington junction, south of Oxford, opened on 24th October 1864. There were intermediate stations at Tiddington, Wheatley, Morris Cowley and Littlemore plus Horspath Halt near the tunnel. A month later the line carried a Royal visitor. On Monday, 21st November, the Prince of Wales plus numerous other dignitaries travelled on the 10.40 am train from London to Thame for a meet of the Earl of Macclesfield's

Dukedog 4-4-0 no 9018 hauls a freight train at Princes Risborough. Photographed on 21st August 1948. (John H. Meredith)

hounds at the Three Pigeons at Milton Common. The party returned by the 2.55 pm train.

The original station at Princes Risborough comprised two short platforms and wooden buildings. The town later had a four-line station with bays at the northern ends of the up and down platforms. Thame station had a wooden all-over roof covering the two platforms and a large goods yard with four sidings on the up side. The branch's broad gauge did not last for long. On 1st February 1867 the Wycombe Railway amalgamated with the Great Western Railway and on 23rd August 1870 the entire line from High Wycombe to Kennington junction closed for conversion to narrow (or standard) gauge. Just over a week later passenger services resumed with goods traffic following after a few days.

By the 1930s passenger traffic was steadily declining and as an economy measure railmotors were introduced between Princes Risborough and Thame. During the Second World War an American Military Hospital was established near

18

Wheatley which meant hospital trains arrived from the East coast ports, often pulled by unfamiliar Great Eastern Railway B12s and D16s. There were times too when the Reading line was obstructed by bombing and expresses for Worcester used the Thame route. In 1941, with many men serving in the forces, women staff were taken on. A woman guard recalled seeing sparks flying out of a locomotive's chimney and, giving it little thought, she later discovered that she had been in charge of an ammunition train!

After the war passenger traffic fell and rumours of closure circulated. On 23rd October 1959 the British Transport Commission (BTC) officially denied the possibility but said that the matter was 'under investigation' – so often a first step to closure. By 1962 the threat was real enough. The BTC reckoned the line was losing £26,000 a year and that at times only a handful of passengers were using it. Finally, after much local indignation, it was announced that passenger services would be withdrawn as from 7th January 1963. The last train comprised five coaches instead of the usual two, hauled by 2-6-2 Prairie tank no 6111. As it left Oxford a nearby diesel gave a farewell salute from its horn. Wheatley's passengers joining the train included a man dressed in deep mourning complete with frock coat and top hat while another dressed as Dr Beeching.

Sections of the track exist today. Since closure freight trains have served Morris Cowley from the Oxford end, and oil traffic has reached Thame from Princes Risborough. Thame station has disappeared with only two platforms' edges remaining.

Princes Risborough to Watlington

The villagers of Watlington had the Earl of Macclesfield, squire of Shirburn Castle, to thank for their branch to Princes Risborough. It was through his persistence, and later his involvement as a director, that in 1869 the independent Watlington & Princes Risborough Railway (W&PRR) Company's Act was passed. Earlier an Act of 1864 had agreed the Wallingford & Watlington Railway but only the portion from Cholsey (then Wallingford Road) to Wallingford was built, opening in 1866. Had it been completed, a through route from the Bristol main line to the Wycombe Railway would have been created. The failure of the scheme much displeased Watlington's residents, including the Earl of Macclesfield.

Work on the Watlington to Princes Risborough branch proceeded at low cost since there was little heavy engineering involved. The standard gauge line, which ran southwest from

Aston Rowant not long before closure. Beyond the station the single track passed under the main London to Oxford A40 road. There are hopes the station will re-open to serve trains from Chinnor plus a weekday link with Chiltern Railways at Princes Risborough. (Lens of Sutton)

20

The terminus at Watlington, July 1949. The station opened in August 1872 with a service of three trains each way daily. Earlier plans to link Watlington with Wallingford never materialised. (Lens of Sutton)

Princes Risborough along the Chilterns foothills, opened on 15th August 1872 with a service of three trains each way daily. There were two intermediate stations at Chinnor and Aston Rowant. Because of the low number of passengers, the independent company soon ran into financial difficulties. The original Princes Risborough station was a small wooden platform just short of the GWR station, so passengers had to walk to change trains, although a goods connection existed. Locomotives and rolling stock were hired from the GWR and it was not long before the independent company's debts could not be paid. An approach was made to the GWR to work the line at an annual rent of £600 but it was refused. The GWR claimed that special locomotives would be required over a branch so lightly constructed – a typical ploy used to run down a line until it could be cheaply acquired. Eventually the GWR obtained powers to purchase the W&PRR by an Act of 1883 at about half the cost it had taken to build the line. Formal transfer took place on 1st June of that year with actual possession going ahead on 31st December.

21

The GWR showed little interest in improving its newly acquired line. A budget of £3,750 was authorised to put it into proper order but nothing much was done. Trackside fencing was occasionally improved but not to a good enough standard for a farmer at Lewknor who demanded a fence high enough to stop his turkeys flying over it! The GWR took over two tank engines and one of these, a 2-4-0 side-tank, received the number 1384 and was rebuilt at Swindon in 1899. After working other GWR branches it passed into the hands of Colonel Stephens for service on the Weston, Clevedon & Portishead Railway. When the locomotive acquired the name *Hesperus*, it was suggested (R. K. Kirkland, *The Railway Magazine*, June 1956) that it was given this name because of some of the wreck-like locomotives on the Colonel's railways!

To encourage local passenger traffic, rail-level halts were opened at Bledlow Bridge, Kingston Crossing and Lewknor Bridge. The halt at Bledlow Bridge was an improvement for the local folk since the earlier Bledlow station on the Oxford line was a mile from the village. As railcars disappeared from GWR stock, ordinary train working resumed and in September 1925 an additional halt was opened at Wainhill Crossing.

Leaving Princes Risborough, the Watlington and Oxford single-track branches ran side-by-side for about half a mile and it was said that timetables were arranged so that trains could not race each other on the two routes. The principal intermediate station was Chinnor with its buildings on the up side, a goods yard and sidings. On the down side, several sidings laid in 1927 served a large lime and cement works and this track still exists. Beyond the rather isolated station of Aston Rowant the line passed under the main London-Oxford road before reaching the terminus, Watlington station, with its single short platform. There was a run-round loop, a goods yard with three sidings and a locomotive shed.

It was inevitable that such a lightly-used line should fall victim to the 'Beeching Axe' despite the many protests of its loyal users. The last journey took place on Saturday, 29th June 1957, when, after 85 years of faithful service, the branch was closed to passengers. Because so many gathered for the event, an extra coach was added but, when the train arrived at Chinnor, this

22

was hardly adequate. The *Thame Gazette* reported, 'After a reasonably good imitation of a rugger scrum, the Parish Council, principal inhabitants and freight were thrust aboard by unseen forces from the rear and the journey commenced.' The proud days of the GWR and the 'Watlington Flyer' have unhappily long since gone.

The Chinnor & Princes Risborough Railway

Happily for rail enthusiasts a section of the former line between Chinnor and Princes Risborough, known as the Icknield Line, has reopened with passenger services running over the 4-mile length along what was once the Watlington branch. The Chinnor and Princes Risborough Railway (C&PRR), formed in 1989, has grand plans for the future. When visited by the author in June

Chinnor station, June 1999. Plans to rebuild the station to its original style are well in hand. (Author)

The Chinnor & Princes Risborough Railway run regular weekend services from Chinnor to Thame Junction. DMU Single Car class 121 awaits departure, June 1999. (Author)

1999 work was well in hand to rebuild Chinnor station, keeping it as near to the original as possible, and a DMU Single Car class 121 was providing a regular passenger service between Chinnor and Thame Junction.

On the platform is a reminder of Cambrian Railway days. The waiting room, booking office and tea rooms have been built using a 100 year old coach body which had spent much of its life in a back garden at Appleton, near Oxford, donated by Mr Jim Heaton. Removal of the coach was not easy. It had to be cut in half, pulled round the side of the house, and brought to Chinnor for rebuilding.

A consideration is also in hand to bring about a joint venture between Chiltern Railways and the C&PRR. Plans include the relaying of track (removed in 1963) between Chinnor and Aston Rowant and the building of a new station at Aston Rowant. This will allow frequent weekday services along the Icknield Line connecting with main line traffic through to London Marylebone

This 100 year old Cambrian coach body at Chinnor serves as a waiting room, ticket office and refreshment room. (Author)

Chinnor c1910. This was the branch's main intermediary station with a goods yard and sidings. Closed to passengers in July 1957, a section of line was re-opened in 1994 by the Chinnor & Princes Risborough Railway. (Lens of Sutton)

Princes Risborough station, June 1999. Formerly a GW&GC jt station, it once provided services to Oxford via Thame, also via Chinnor to Watlington. (Author)

while the C&PRR will continue to run heritage trains at weekends and Bank Holidays.

2
The Metropolitan Railway

*Baker Street/Rickmansworth/Aylesbury/
Verney Junction and branches to Stanmore,
Uxbridge, Watford and Chesham*

*Metropolitan and Piccadilly trains at Rayners Lane on the Uxbridge branch
probably in the early 1930s. The 'Met' coaches can be found today at the
Bluebell Railway in Sussex. (John H. Meredith)*

In the 1850s London's streets were frequently jammed with slow-
moving traffic and it was left to a City solicitor, Charles Pearson,
to find a solution. This came with the advent of a railway to be
built below the surface of the streets although raising capital
proved a major problem. Part of this came from the Great

A C13 class locomotive no 67418 hauling LTE passenger set no 2 waits at Chesham station. Photograph taken August 1951, shortly before electrification of the line. (John H. Meredith)

Western Railway (GWR) which had more than a passing interest in the project since it saw a means to get its trains from Paddington through to the City. In 1853 the Metropolitan Railway Company (MET) was formed. There was immediate concern from residents that tunnels would collapse or that passengers would be asphyxiated! Despite such fears a 3½ mile line was constructed between Bishop's Road (Paddington) and Farringdon Street and the world's first underground railway opened on 10th January 1863. The following year trains reached Hammersmith and Kensington, today known as Kensington (Olympia).

With steam trains working the line, the tunnels soon became heavily coated with soot and the persistent smoke upset staff and passengers alike. Staff were given permission to grow beards as a protection against the fumes! By the time City lines were completed, the MET had looked further afield and, anticipating lucrative goods and passenger traffic beyond Finchley Road, a line was built outwards from Baker Street. St John's Wood and

An early picture at Wendover taken as a Metropolitan E class locomotive passes under Station Bridge. Trains reached Wendover and on to Aylesbury in 1892. (Lens of Sutton)

Swiss Cottage were reached by 1868 and Willesden Green by 1879 – after Finchley Road tracks were mostly overground. The next objective was Harrow-on-the-Hill where a station opened on 2nd August 1880. There were 36 trains daily to and from Baker Street plus a generous Sunday service.

The directors continued to extend the MET with the Chilterns next in their sights. To achieve this, the Harrow & Rickmans-worth Railway was incorporated in 1874 with trains reaching Rickmansworth on 1st September 1887. Looking outwards again, the next place of any importance was Chesham which MET trains reached on 8th July 1889. The branch from Chalfont Road (renamed Chalfont & Latimer in November 1915) was built as a single line. Chesham welcomed the trains and donated £2,000 towards the cost of a station to ensure it would reach the town centre and not the outskirts as originally planned. A reminder of the branch's earlier days can be found with a visit to the Bluebell Railway at Sheffield Park in Sussex where a 'Chesham set' of coaches can be seen.

Northwood station on the former Metropolitan & Great Central joint line between Harrow and Rickmansworth. Posters offered passengers 'a region of green hillsides and woods where houses are plentiful'. (Lens of Sutton)

As expected, Aylesbury was the next destination to be reached with services commencing on 1st September 1892. To the north of Aylesbury a further line had been opened in 1868 by a company called the Aylesbury & Buckingham Railway (A&BR) with its single line worked by the GWR. The railway started from a junction on the Oxford to Bletchley line (later to be known as Verney Junction) to reach Aylesbury via Quainton Road. Traffic was initially almost non-existent since Verney Junction was isolated in a very rural locality without even a small village. The MET however saw an opportunity and took over the line in 1891, doubling the track by 1897.

Another remote MET outpost was yet to come. The Brill branch, previously known as the Wotton Tramway, had opened in 1871 with the possibility envisaged in an Act of 1883 that it might eventually reach Oxford (see chapter 6). Although this never came about, the MET foresaw a lucrative branch should it be completed. On 1st December 1899 the Oxford and Aylesbury Tramroad (O&AT), as it optimistically became known, made over the working of the line to the MET,

Ex LNER (GCR) class A5 4-6-2T (as BR 69807) waiting in a bay at Rickmansworth to take over a MET train to Aylesbury. (Barry Hoper)

the O&AT remaining the proprietors.

An important event in the history of the MET came in 1899 when the Great Central Railway (GCR) opened a line between Rugby and Quainton Road. The Chairman, Sir Edward Watkin, planned to link the North and Midlands with London and eventually, he hoped, on to Paris (see chapter 5). Sir Edward no doubt considered that a union with the MET would provide the ready-made link he required but the MET was not happy about the finances of the GCR and a joint company never materialised. Instead the GCR was granted running powers over MET tracks between Quainton Road and Harrow-on-the-Hill but the MET refused to allow any GCR trains south of Harrow. The problem was solved when the MET built separate tracks and leased them to the GCR for its exclusive use to and from Marylebone.

On 4th July 1904, the MET opened a branch from Harrow-on-the-Hill to Uxbridge which sparked off a considerable building

Staff pose proudly on the up-platform at Rickmansworth MET station, c1910. In 1925 electrification reached Rickmansworth and the station became an electric and steam locomotive change-over point. (Lens of Sutton)

boom in the general area. A local newspaper commented, 'Uxbridge is expected to grow into a first-class residential neighbourhood and health resort. Houses will be available from £500 freehold'. An intermediate station on the branch was opened at Ruislip and numerous halts were opened at various times to encourage traffic into the sparse countryside. In 1910, partly to overcome bitter rivalry between the MET and the District line, a spur was built from a halt at Rayners Lane (opened in May 1906) to connect with the District line at South Harrow although initially it was used solely to carry coal to a gasworks. The line subsequently carried District (later Piccadilly line) trains to Uxbridge with running powers over the MET tracks. An unusual aspect of the spur was that, although owned by the MET, it never carried any MET trains.

There was a spectacular accident on 23rd December 1904 when a north-bound parcels train from Marylebone, hauled by a Robinson 4-4-0 no 1040, left the track at Aylesbury. It was a foggy night and the train entered the station travelling at such a

London Transport locomotive L44 (now Metropolitan 1 at Quainton Road) at Rickmansworth in 1950. In the background, one of the Metropolitan electric locomotives used to haul trains from Rickmansworth to Baker Street or beyond. (Barry Hoper)

speed that it derailed and mounted the platform. Immediately an up Manchester train ploughed into the wreckage, fortunately at a slow speed and little extra damage was done. The parcels train driver died later in hospital. One of the vans had been loaded with Christmas puddings and it was reported that some of the people of Aylesbury lent more than a willing hand in helping to clear the line.

Electrification came to the MET on 1st January 1905 when the first multiple-unit service began between Baker Street and Harrow, also serving the Harrow to Uxbridge branch. The first cars were built by the Metropolitan Amalgamated Carriage & Wagon Company. These cars compared well with the earlier narrow compartments used on the MET which had often been described as 'knee-knockers'. The first ten electric locomotives, 'camel-back' types each carried on two motor bogies, were built

London Transport locomotive L44 heads a passenger set at Chalfont & Latimer station, August 1951. (John H. Meredith)

between 1904 and 1906. A further ten of the same type, capable of handling heavier main line trains, were purchased in 1907 from British Thomson Houston (BTH). To allow working over non-electrified lines, these were changed for steam locomotives at Wembley Park or Harrow.

As services improved, demand on the electric locomotives grew. Batches were withdrawn from 1922 and sent to Vickers Ltd at Barrow-in-Furness for reconstruction, returning with very little of the original remaining. Immediate needs were met when new locomotives were delivered, having four 300 hp motors, two in each bogie, giving 1,200 hp in all. They were painted chocolate and lined in black and yellow. The locomotives could attain a maximum speed of 65 mph and were capable of fast acceleration from rest. They initially carried the word 'Metropolitan' between two coats of arms but later the word was replaced by a bronze plate bearing the name of a well known character associated with the MET. There were eventually 20 locomotives and only no 15 was different, being called *Wembley 1924* to commemorate the exhibition, where it was shown with one side removed to display

Great Missenden station, c1910. This was in an area that became known as 'Metroland'. In the 1930s quality houses cost under £1,000. (Lens of Sutton)

the internal equipment. On 5th January 1925 electrification reached Rickmansworth, with the station becoming an electric and steam locomotive change-over point.

For many years the MET had been aware that Watford, although already served by the LNWR (chapter 3), had sufficient potential to justify another rail service to London. Parliamentary approval was obtained in 1922 although construction proved difficult with some ten bridges required including two across the Grand Union Canal and the river Colne. The cost of the branch was put at £300,000. The line opened on 2nd November 1925 with electric trains worked by the MET and steam-hauled trains by the LNER (formerly GCR). Almost immediately there were around 140 trains daily. The futility of running steam trains over electric tracks was soon appreciated so the LNER withdrew its services after the General Strike of May 1926. Much publicity was given to the Watford branch – 'The New Metro Route to Watford is now open for traffic, offering many advantages to the travelling public. It makes Watford – Hertfordshire's largest and most important town – easier of access; opens up an unique

Aylesbury station in steam days. To the left a 4-4-0 GCR Director class locomotive and beyond a Metropolitan H class. (Lens of Sutton)

residential district offering unlimited scope for building operations and, at the same time, materially improves London's transport facilities'.

A link was constructed between the intermediate station of Croxley and Rickmansworth so that Watford trains could work northwards without reversing and also allow a shuttle service of electric trains between Rickmansworth and Watford. There was concern that the MET's Watford terminus was in a quiet part of the town so four 28-seater buses were purchased to meet trains and take passengers to the town centre. In October 1927 the MET made a further attempt to reach the centre of Watford by purchasing a property at 44, Watford High Street, formerly the Empress Tea Rooms, for £14,200. A costly tunnel of approximately 1,100 yards would have been necessary and the project was abandoned. The building, recently a Grange furniture store, more recently became a branch of Next Ltd.

Late in the life of the MET there were plans to build a further

Track work at Aylesbury in pre-grouping days. The station also served a branch to Princes Risborough which opened in 1863. (Lens of Sutton)

branch to Stanmore and on to Elstree linking with the former Midland line from St Pancras. Only the 4½ mile stretch to Stanmore was completed, opening in December 1932, leaving the main line half a mile north of Wembley Park station. Intermediate stations were built at Kingsbury and Canons Park, with Queensbury following in December 1934. A service of 144 trains daily was provided to attract passengers and many trains travelled the 6½ miles between Wembley Park and Baker Street nonstop. When in November 1939 a connection with the Bakerloo line was completed, Stanmore's MET trains were withdrawn and replaced by 'tube' trains to and from the Elephant & Castle. In May 1979 the Jubilee line opened between Charing Cross and Baker Street, and Wembley Park to Stanmore became a part of it.

On 1st July 1933 the MET passed into the ownership of the London Passenger Transport Board (LPTB). Locomotives, including the handsome K class engines, were repainted with the London Transport lettering and they continued their freight and passenger workings up to Verney Junction. During the years

Winslow Road, a remote station on the line from Quainton Road to Verney Junction, the Metropolitan's furthest outpost. Winslow Road closed in July 1936 to subsequently become 'Station Kennels'. (Lens of Sutton)

up to the Second World War the MET as it was known slowly began to disintegrate. The Brill branch closed on 30th November 1935 and the line from Quainton Road to Verney Junction was reduced to single track and kept only for goods traffic. There were many incidents during the air raids, mostly in the City section. Moorgate station was practically destroyed and bombs hit the tunnels putting the line between Euston Square and King's Cross out of action for many weeks. There was also heavy damage at Baker Street and Kilburn. First-class facilities were withdrawn.

On 1st January 1948, nationalisation meant that railways previously administered by the LPTB became part of the British Transport Commission (BTC). On 1st January 1963 a further change took place when the BTC was dissolved, its place taken by the new British Railways Board, with the London Underground under independent control (the London Transport Board). On 12th September 1960 electric trains reached Amersham and Chesham and on 9th September 1961, the last day of steam working on the London Transport, MET services were withdrawn north of Amersham. By June 1962 four-tracking had been completed as far north as Watford South junction. On 3rd September 1966 the last train ran on the former GCR line from Aylesbury to Rugby and the last vestige of Sir Edward Watkin's dream of a line to the south coast had gone. Aylesbury became an outpost of the former MET line served only by local diesel services from Marylebone via Rickmansworth or via High Wycombe.

July 1989 was the centenary of the opening of the MET line between Rickmansworth and Chesham, and E class 0-4-4T Metropolitan 1 hauled a number of special trains between Watford and Chesham carrying a headboard reading 'Chesham 100 Years 1889 – 1989'. Beyond Aylesbury there are still many reminders of the past. The platform edges have survived at Waddesdon Manor (closed in July 1936) and at Quainton Road the many fine exhibits at the Buckinghamshire Railway Centre include Metropolitan 1 (chapter 5). Grandborough Road's platform edges can also be determined and at Winslow Road the site became 'Station Kennels'.

At Verney Junction there is little to see except surviving platform edges and the single freight line that runs from Bicester to Bletchley. Station House is still there carrying the date 1870 and the station ticket office has become a private garage. Nearby is *The Verney Arms* which opened in the 1890s as the *Station Hotel.* When visiting the area in June 1999 it seemed hard to believe that this was once a junction serving four different directions and where it was once possible to book excursions to such places as Ramsgate.

3
'Lord Ebury's Line'
Watford to Rickmansworth

LNWR locomotives at Watford Junction station c1919. The leading engine is 2-4-0 no 193 'Rocket', a Precedent class locomotive built about 1890. The second is 4-4-0 no 1957 rebuilt as a 2 cylinder Renown class 2P. (Barry Hoper)

The Watford & Rickmansworth Railway (W&RR) was originally the brainchild of Lord Ebury who saw it as a means to connect a newly opened GWR Uxbridge branch with the LNWR at Watford. He obtained Parliamentary approval in 1860 but due to financial problems, the section between Rickmansworth and Uxbridge was never completed. Instead the W&RR comprised a

The LNWR Croxley Green station, c1910, was at one time a grand affair. In March 1913 the station and buildings were totally destroyed by a fire started by suffragettes. (Lens of Sutton)

4½ mile branch from Rickmansworth to Watford Junction.

When the first train arrived at Rickmansworth from Watford on 1st October 1862 hundreds of people were there to welcome it. The town's original station was a basic wooden construction reported to be 'flimsy and leaky'. Just beyond the station, trains crossed the Grand Union Canal. The W&RR Act had decreed that the bridge should be 'good and substantial' and 'at least 10 feet over the top water level'. Initially the branch carried five trains each way daily on weekdays only and the only intermediate station was at the southern end of Watford High Street. The push-pull two-coach trains were hauled by 0-6-2 freight tank locomotives and were kept busy with both passengers and goods.

The W&RR was operated from the outset by the LNWR which paid the independent company 'a sum equal to 50% of the amount of the gross earnings from tolls, rates etc' until the LNWR took over the line completely on 27th June 1881. In addition to the considerable sidings traffic on the branch, the

Croxley station on the Metropolitan line from Rickmansworth to Watford. There are proposals that, at some future date, Croxley will be an intermediate station on a line linking the MET line with Watford Junction. (Lens of Sutton)

carriage of watercress developed and it became a common sight to see hampers being transported to the market at Watford and stock used on the branch acquired the nickname 'watercress trains'.

In 1912 a new branch opened between Watford and Croxley Green. Steam passenger service commenced on 15th June with freight traffic starting on 1st October. Trains left the W&RR line at Croxley Green junction with part of the branch doubled for the extra traffic. During February 1913, track was laid from Bushey & Oxhey station joining the W&RR just south of Watford High Street station (known as the 'new line') and another loop, forming a triangle, allowed steam trains from Euston to run directly to Croxley Green. On 10th March 1913 Croxley Green station was temporarily put out of action when destroyed by a fire, said to have been started deliberately by suffragettes.

Electric trains reached Watford from Euston on 10th July 1922 and an electric service to Croxley Green started on 30th October 1922. On the W&RR branch, Rickmansworth's wooden station

42

A deserted Watford High Street station on the branch from Watford Junction to Croxley Green. (Lens of Sutton)

Closure of the Rickmansworth branch passed relatively uneventfully on 2nd March 1952 with only a handful of enthusiasts on the last train. Here, earlier the same day an Oerlikon set awaits departure to Watford. (John H. Meredith)

Rickmansworth (Church Street) station in the early 1960s after closure to passenger traffic. Goods traffic survived until January 1967. Today the site has been cleared and comprises a block of flats called St Mary's Court. (Lens of Sutton)

was replaced by a brick building but passengers at the terminus had to wait until 26th September 1927 for an electric service, by which time it had become a London, Midland & Scottish Railway (LMS) branch. It was found that full-sized electric cars used on both the Croxley Green and Rickmansworth branches put an excessive load on the local sub-station. The result was that they were replaced by nine coaches from ex-LNWR/London Electric Railway tube stock when these were withdrawn from the Euston-Watford route in 1930/31. When Watford Football Club was playing at home extra coaches were often added. On 4th December 1982, a new station, known as Watford Stadium Halt, was opened to serve supporters. The then chairman of the Watford Football Club, Elton John, and Lord Aberdare, chairman of the Football Trust, performed the ceremony.

During the 1920s competition from bus services made itself felt. In 1921 the Rickmansworth & District Omnibus Company began operating services to Watford although the company did

44

Watford High Street station in LNWR days c1910. The station opened on 1st October 1862 with six trains on the Rickmansworth branch each way daily. (Lens of Sutton)

not last. It was replaced by the National Omnibus & Transport Company which extended its services from Croxley Green to Rickmansworth in 1924. The Lewis Omnibus Company followed, operating from Rickmansworth to Watford and St Albans. This company also took over the Metropolitan (MET) bus service from Watford MET station to the town centre.

There were further problems when a new branch was opened in 1925 for MET trains from Rickmansworth via Croxley to Watford. When services began on November 2nd, 35 MET electric trains daily were reaching Baker Street (and Aldgate in peak hours) plus the same number of steam trains to and from Marylebone. The LMS, with its Croxley Green branch, considered this new branch superfluous but the MET countered saying that the LMS Croxley Green station was at least half a mile from the village and serving nobody. The MET claimed that the station stood like 'a pelican in the wilderness'.

Nine tube coaches introduced in 1930/31 on the Rickmansworth to Watford Junction branch were replaced in 1939 by

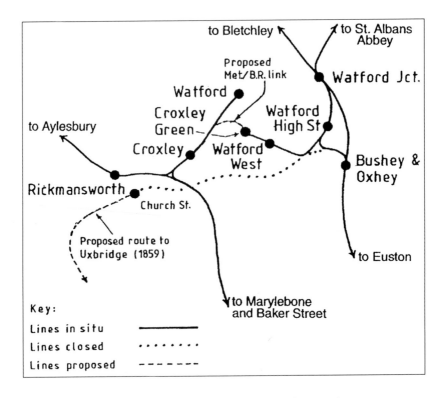

spare main line stock. These were Oerlikon saloon car sets, already 20 years old, and they were used on the branch until its closure in 1952. The last train from Rickmansworth (renamed Rickmansworth Church Street in September 1950) ran on 2nd March 1952. As the 10.45 pm to Watford made its final run, only a dozen or so railway enthusiasts were carried plus one 'bona fide' passenger. The 'right away' was given and the lights of 'Ricky' were quickly left behind. Crossing the canal, the train gathered speed up to Tolpits Farm, passed Brightwells Farm and then rattled down to Croxley Green junction, pausing for the staff to be handed up to the box for the last time from a passenger train. One bereaved enthusiast remarked, 'It was a quiet funeral'.

The track lasted another 15 years with the occasional goods train working the spur down to Dickinson's Croxley Mills or

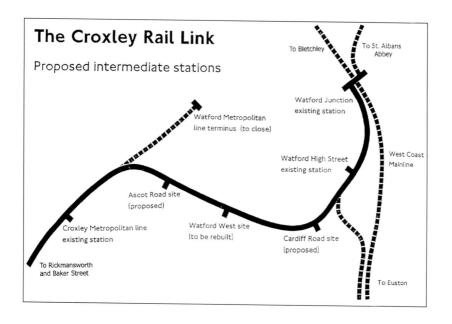

The Croxley Rail Link

Proposed intermediate stations

To Bletchley

To St. Albans Abbey

Watford Junction existing station

Watford Metropolitan line terminus (to close)

West Coast Mainline

Watford High Street existing station

Ascot Road site (proposed)

Croxley Metropolitan line existing station

Watford West site (to be rebuilt)

Cardiff Road site (proposed)

To Rickmansworth and Baker Street

To Euston

possibly shunting in the Universal Asbestos factory sidings. At Brightwells Farm another siding led to the Colne Valley Water Company's sidings where a 2 ft gauge light railway was built in 1932. Not far from Watford High Street station another siding served Benskins Brewery with tracks reaching its four-storeyed malthouse plus a short spur to the boiler and brewhouse. The last rail despatch of beer left in 1953 although barley was delivered by rail until 1956. Freight services on the Rickmansworth branch lasted until 2nd January 1967 when the line closed completely.

The Metropolitan service survives between Rickmansworth and Watford, also trains still run between Watford High Street and Croxley Green. But all this could be changing during the next decade. For some years plans have been under consideration to link the Metropolitan branch to the Croxley Green branch by building a railway bridge over the A412 Watford Road near the Grand Union Canal at Cassiobridge. In this way Metropolitan line trains would be linked to Watford High Street and Watford Junction stations. The plans include a new station in

47

Ascot Road near the Croxley Business Park. The proposals would mean closure of the existing Croxley Green station and the Watford Metropolitan station. Although the scheme has local council support, confirmation was still awaited during 1999 that funds to carry out the work would be provided by London Underground and Railtrack. The scheme has been in existence since the early 1990s and there is little optimism there will be a speedy result. When Parliamentary approval was given in 1860 to link Rickmansworth with Watford by rail, trains were running within two years!

4
LNWR Cross Country Routes

Bletchley/Verney Junction/Banbury and Verney Junction/Oxford

Class 2F LMS 0-6-0 no 3195 seen at Bletchley on 19th April 1930. Initially known as a 1798 class locomotive, it was built at Derby in 1888 to designs of S. W. Johnson. (Barry Hoper)

Bletchley/Verney Junction/Banbury

The small market town of Buckingham was unfortunate since, during the earlier days of 'railway mania', it was overlooked by the main railway companies and transport facilities remained

Buckingham station not long before closure in the 1960s. When a branch from Bletchley via Buckingham to Banbury was opened by the Buckingham Railway on 1st May 1850, there were great celebrations in the town. (Lens of Sutton)

Only a bare platform edge survives today at the former Fulwell & Westbury station. Double track was intended between Verney Junction and Banbury but due to financial troubles only single track was built. (Lens of Sutton)

Banbury (Merton Street) station opened on 1st May 1850 as the northern terminus of the Buckingham Railway. The locomotive, seen here around 1950, was an ex-LMS 2-6-4T designed by W. A. Stanier and introduced in 1935. (Lens of Sutton)

Swanbourne station between Bletchley and Verney Junction survives today and there are hopes trains might use the line once again. (Author)

At Swanbourne the owner of the station building, Michael Waters, has created this locomotive in his hedge. It has had much publicity including a picture in the Daily Telegraph. (Author)

This oil lamp at Swanbourne came originally from Verney Junction station. Swanbourne station closed to regular passenger traffic on 1st January 1968. (Author)

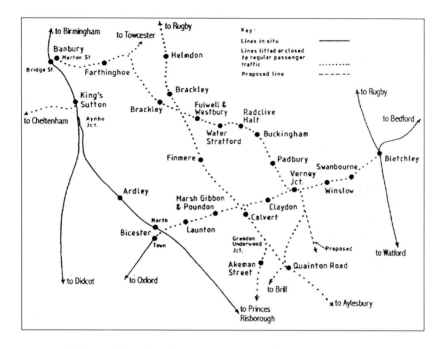

poor. When the London & Birmingham Railway (L&BR) completed its line in September 1838, Buckingham was bypassed with the nearest station about ten miles away at Bletchley. It was mainly thanks to the efforts of the Duke of Buckingham and Sir Harry Verney that the Buckingham Railway came about. It consisted of a line from Bletchley to Banbury and another from Verney Junction to Oxford. It was decided that the railway to Banbury should receive priority and it was not long before the construction sites around Buckingham became a 'hard drinking and riotous centre'. It was so bad that the directors had to bring in a full time chaplain and several scripture readers in an attempt to calm things down!

Construction between Bletchley and Banbury took just under three years. There were periods of financial difficulty and instead of the double track intended, single track was built. Four trains ran each way daily, worked by the LNWR. When the line opened to passengers on 1st May 1850 there were great celebrations with many people at Banbury to watch the 6.30 am train depart. The

Verney Junction station was at one time the furthest outpost of the Metropolitan Railway. Apart from MET trains, it also served lines to Bletchley, Banbury and Oxford. (Lens of Sutton)

All that remains of Verney Junction today is a grass-covered freight line and the platform edges. Nearby is privately owned 'Station House' where the garage was once the ticket office. (Author)

The Verney Arms, close to Verney Junction station, opened in the 1890s and was known as Station Hotel. It is named after Lord Verney who, with the Duke of Buckingham, did much to establish the local railway. (Author)

station was gaily decorated with flags, there were booths and stalls and, throughout the day, a brass band played. Later that year, on 1st October, the line to Oxford opened as far as Islip, extended to a temporary station at Oxford Road on 2nd December and on 20th May 1851 opened throughout. The opportunity was immediately seized to run excursions to the Great Exhibition in London's Hyde Park and when a special train left Oxford on 21st May, there were ten coaches carrying some 400 passengers.

Travelling the line from Bletchley, the first intermediate station on the line towards Verney Junction was Swanbourne, although the village was over a mile away. Despite its remoteness, the station at its peak boasted takings averaging £400 a week. The station building has survived the years and a lamp in the adjacent garden came from Verney Junction station. The hedge nearby has been cut to resemble a steam locomotive complete with wheels! The next station was Winslow which, before Verney Junction station opened in 1868, was an important place for changing between the Banbury and Oxford routes. For this reason sizeable waiting rooms were built on the up side. The station, demolished in the 1990s, had a spacious approach road with a circular drive around a green. Verney Junction with its three platforms served not only the Buckingham Railway but, from 1868, it became a terminus for trains from Aylesbury via Quainton Road (chapter 2).

Verney Junction to Oxford

Towards Oxford, the next intermediate station was Claydon where only a platform edge gives evidence of past activities. The last major station was at Bicester in Oxfordshire. This became Bicester London Road in 1954 and when it closed in 1968 it seemed this was the end. Yet today, known as Bicester Town, passenger trains call once again with three-coach DMUs

Looking towards Verney Junction at Claydon, June 1999. All that remains is the platform edge, a single-track cross-country freight line and a level crossing. The nearby pillar-box still reads 'Claydon station'. (Author)

Launton station, between Verney Junction and Bicester. In the early 1920s, six trains stopped at Launton each way daily. (Lens of Sutton)

Claydon station in the 1960s on the line from Verney Junction to Bicester. Freight traffic came to an end in January 1964 and passenger services closed in January 1968. (Lens of Sutton)

Bicester (London Road) station in the 1960s. Bicester has two stations, the other known today as Bicester North on the former GWR route from Princes Risborough to Banbury. (Lens of Sutton)

When Bicester London Road closed in 1968 it seemed to be the end but in 1989 services to Oxford recommenced. The station is today known as Bicester Town and DMUs provide a regular service to Oxford. (Author)

providing trains daily to Oxford, a service jointly funded by local councils and Network South East. A plaque on the single platform reads, 'Councillor Bryan Duggan, Chairman of Oxford-shire County Council, unveiled this plaque on 13th May 1989'.

Travelling the route from Verney Junction to Banbury, all that could be found at the former Padbury station was an old sleeper in the grass and a bulldog which took exception to the author! At Buckingham the station site has become a wooded walk with the platform edge just visible in the grass. No trace could be found of either Radclive or Water Stratford halts (opened in August 1956) whereas at Fulwell & Westbury, the trackbed passed a line of poplars and towards Banbury stood a crossing keeper's house. A local tractor-driver reminisced over the joys of once travelling such a picturesque line.

Passenger traffic over the two routes was never very heavy although goods traffic proved useful. When the motor bus provided competition and then the private motor car in the 1920s and 1930s, passenger levels dropped. In 1952 BR reduced the service but traffic increased once again when lightweight single-unit diesel cars were introduced in 1956 between Banbury and Buckingham. Despite this, BR claimed that the section remained uneconomic and closure came on 2nd January 1961. The line between Buckingham and Verney Junction survived a further three years to finally close on 7th September 1964. The line from Bicester to Bletchley fared little better, closing on 1st January 1968. When the last train ran it was nearly empty and only a few exploding detonators marked the closure.

There is currently local speculation that the stretch from Bletchley to Claydon may reopen as a test track for signalling and that by the year 2004 it may link Bletchley with Bicester to provide a useful east-west rail link. But much would need to be done rebuilding stations and restoring track where it has been vandalised.

5
Northwards To Rugby
And Steam At
Quainton Road

Quainton Road/Calvert/Brackley/Woodford/
Rugby/Grendon Underwood junction/
Ashendon junction
The Buckinghamshire Railway Centre

A road overbridge at the former Waddesdon Manor station between Quainton Road and Aylesbury, June 1999. The station has been demolished but the platform edge is just visible under the bridge. (Author)

Quainton Road/Calvert/Brackley/ Woodford/Rugby

The Manchester, Sheffield & Lincolnshire Railway (MS&LR) began its existence as a provincial company providing a link across the Pennines and reaching Grimsby to the east. Its chairman, Sir Edward Watkin, was an ambitious man for, by the end of the 1880s, he was also serving as chairman to the Metropolitan, South Eastern and East London Railways. One of his aims was to build a route to reach London from the MS&LR to run from Annesley, north of Nottingham, to Quainton Road, north of Aylesbury. At this point it would join existing tracks (later absorbed by the Metropolitan Railway) to reach the London terminus of Marylebone.

Milk churns at Calvert around the turn of the 19th century. Calvert was a busy station on the direct GCR route from Marylebone to Rugby and beyond. (Lens of Sutton)

The remains of Calvert station today, which closed completely in 1964. The only 'visitors' are occasional waste trains from London destined for a nearby landfill site. (Author)

The section from Rugby to Quainton Road, almost 40 miles in length, received Parliamentary approval at a second attempt on 28th March 1893. The line was expensive to build requiring some 5,000 men, 150 horses, 50 locomotives and 1,700 wagons. South of Brackley a 252 yard viaduct was needed to cross the Great Ouse valley. The line was clearly a gamble particularly since the MS&LR was forever short of finance. Indeed the reputation of the company gave rise to rumours that the initials MS&L stood for 'money sunk and lost'. In 1897 the MS&LR changed its name to the Great Central Railway (GCR).

The Quainton Road/Rugby line opened to passenger traffic on 15th March 1899 but it soon disappointed its promoters. Trains ran through thinly-populated agricultural areas and, in consequence, they were usually lightly loaded and few in number. Initially there were twelve passenger trains each way daily with

A general view of Brackley's GCR station, c1910. Brackley's first station was opened by the LNWR in 1850 but the GCR line took away much of the LNWR traffic with its faster route to London when its passenger services commenced in 1899. (Lens of Sutton)

four each way on Sundays. A typical express from London Marylebone covering the route was the 6.20 pm which reached Nottingham (126½ miles) in 1 hour 45 minutes, slipping a coach at Leicester.

The GCR benefited in 1900 with the appointment of J. G. Robinson as locomotive designer and the company came to possess some fine engines. His first was a class 9J 0-6-0 used for goods traffic and this was followed by class 11B 4-4-0 for express passenger trains. Perhaps his best known locomotive was the class 11E 4-4-0 of 1913 known as the *Director*. Two years later Sam Fay was appointed as general manager and he soon earned much respect. By 1920 there were up to nine expresses daily each way between London and Nottingham with at least four including restaurant cars. The GCR earned a good reputation for punctuality and speed, beating the LNWR run to Rugby by

Brackley's Central station building in June 1999, almost 40 years after closure. The property is today an ATS motoring centre and to the south the once well known viaduct has been demolished. (Author)

two minutes and the Midland Railway to Leicester by four minutes.

When 'grouping' came in 1923 the GCR became part of the London & North Eastern Railway (LNER) which provided A3 'Pacifics' to haul its express trains. As steam trains came to an end many kinds of locomotives could be seen including Royal Scot 4-4-0s, Stanier Black 5s plus BR standard class 4 2-6-0s and class 5 4-6-0s. Occasionally a Britannia Pacific could be seen. In 1965 diesel multiple train units were introduced between Nottingham and London with extra trains between Woodford and Nottingham. On Sundays only one train ran in each direction. Freight traffic was considerable with much of it coal from the East Midlands. At Woodford there were as many as 33 sidings for northbound traffic and ten for the south.

By the early 1960s doubts were being raised over the future

Rugby's LNWR northern platform during the First World War. Rugby's Central line station, although some distance from the town centre, was nearby but this finally closed to passengers on 5th May 1969. (Lens of Sutton)

of the line. BR claimed a 'deteriorating financial position' while an ASLEF meeting in August 1962 passed a strongly worded protest to the Minister of Transport asking that complete closure should be refuted. Allegations were made that the government was deliberately running down the line so that it could be closed. When the Beeching Report was announced, the end was in sight. Last minute attempts were made to gain a reprieve but there was no hope and the Minister, Mrs Barbara Castle, made her decision. The last train ran on Saturday, 3rd September 1966.

Brackley station building became an ATS motoring centre but to the south the once-great viaduct has been demolished. At Finmere a road underbridge has survived and tracks still pass through Calvert, where nearby pits are filled with rubbish from much of the south of England. It is ironic that some of the waste comes from the tip covering the Bluebell Railway's East Grinstead proposed extension. Calvert's island platform is still

Quainton Road station on the former GCR line from Rugby to Marylebone closed to regular passenger traffic in 1963. The freight-only main line is currently used to take waste to a landfill site at Calvert. (Author)

there but where buildings once stood it is grass covered. From Calvert a spur still exists, put in during the Second World War, enabling freight to join the Oxford-Bletchley line. Quainton Road has become well known as the headquarters of the Buckingham-shire Railway.

The GCR line to Rugby began as Sir Edward Watkin's dream of a rapid link between the Midlands, the Channel ports — and beyond. It has been suggested more than once that the route should be reopened to provide a fast through route between the Midlands and the Channel Tunnel. If that were to come about, then Sir Edward Watkin's dream would indeed have come true.

Grendon Underwood junction/ Ashendon junction

On 20th November 1905 a 6 mile double-track line opened to goods traffic between Grendon Underwood junction and Ashendon junction, connecting the GCR line with the Great Western & Great Central joint line north of Princes Risborough. Over four months later, on 2nd April 1906, the line opened to passengers. The route via High Wycombe gave the GCR easier access to the capital, with a straighter track and with lesser gradients than on the Metropolitan line & GCR joint line via Aylesbury. In addition staff on the Metropolitan route had frequently obstructed GCR workings. However, little traffic

After closure of Wotton station, formerly on the GCR link between Ashendon junction and Grendon Underwood junction, the building housed chickens! It was later converted to a private residence called 'The Old Station'. (Author)

The Buckinghamshire Railway Centre, founded by volunteers in 1969, is split in two by the 'freight-only' line. Efforts continue with Railtrack to establish a connection with the through line plus the hope to eventually run trains to Aylesbury and beyond. (Author)

resulted on the diversion and the Grendon/Ashendon line closed to passengers in December 1953.

Between Grendon Underwood junction and Ashendon junction, track has survived only as far as a fertilizer plant at Woodham close to where Akeman Street station once stood. Akeman Street station has gone and only the stationmaster's house remains. After closure, Wotton station (GCR) building to the south became derelict and in the 1970s it housed chickens. The building has been subsequently restored to become a private dwelling called appropriately 'The Old Station'. The adjacent stationmaster's house is today 'The Station House'. This was also the area where the GCR track crossed the Wotton Tramway (see chapter 6) with that station's stables only a short distance away.

On Saturday, June 26th 1999, the London Railway Club celebrated its centenary by running a Chiltern Railways turbo diesel train from Marylebone to Quainton Road. (Author)

The Buckinghamshire Railway Centre

Quainton Road station was at one time an outpost of London Transport, when Metropolitan trains ran from Baker Street through Quainton Road to Verney Junction. When the station first opened in 1868 it was part of the Aylesbury & Buckingham Railway which was taken over by the Metropolitan in 1891 (Chapter 2). The station's existing buildings were constructed in 1896. Yet Quainton Road had another important role. The line was also part of the Great Central Railway (GCR) which from 1899 carried main-line trains between the Midlands and London Marylebone. A third line also played a role at Quainton Road. The wooden building standing on platforms 2 and 3 was once a shelter for passengers waiting for trams on the Wotton Tramway

69

Ex-GWR locomotive L99 0-6-0PT, restored and based at Quainton Road, is in frequent use hauling ex-BR Mk 1 coaches at weekends. (Phil Marsh)

– a private system, opened in 1871 for the Duke of Buckingham's estate and by 1872 trams had reached Brill (chapter 6). Initially there was no direct connection between the tramway and Quainton Road although a turntable did connect with a siding. A bay platform (which is today Quainton Road's platform 3) was provided in 1896 for the branch. Like the line to Verney Junction, the tramway also became part of the Metropolitan.

The Buckinghamshire Railway Centre was started by the London Railway Preservation Society in 1969. Items of historical railway equipment were collected and temporarily stored at government depots at Luton and Bishop's Stortford prior to that date but space soon became a problem and a new and permanent home was needed. Many sites were visited and eventually Quainton Road station with its two large goods yards was selected. Quainton Road station closed to passengers on 4th

Metropolitan Railway class E 0-4-4T no 1, the only survivor of a class of seven engines, heads LNWR 1st class dining car at the Buckinghamshire Railway Centre at Quainton Road. (T. Davey)

March 1963 and just over three years later, on 3rd September 1966, the whole line from Aylesbury to Rugby was closed with Quainton Road keeping only its former 'up' line as far as Calvert junction. In 1969, to protect members, Quainton Railway Society Ltd was formed and the London Railway Preservation Society was formally incorporated into the society on 24th April 1971. It is this society that was granted charitable status the following year and is known as the Buckinghamshire Railway Centre.

When the society first moved to the site there was much to be done. No covered accommodation was available so a building was erected in the 'down' yard spanning three 150 ft long tracks to include workshops, a museum and a mess room. At the same time a building was acquired from London Transport, dismantled and transported from Wembley Park, and re-erected at the southern end of the yard. This became known as 'the Wembley Shed' and is used to house relics awaiting restoration

71

and sometimes for special exhibitions. More buildings and exhibits followed, including a 60 ft turntable.

The society's present stock list is formidable. As well as many industrial locomotives, there are about a dozen main line locomotives with a number either undergoing overhaul or away on loan elsewhere. One of the locomotives at Quainton Road is Metropolitan 1, the only survivor of its class. The locomotive, an E class 0-4-4T, saw many years of duty on the MET line although when the MET electrification programme was completed such engines were less necessary. It hauled its last passenger train in 1961 (as London Transport L44) and in 1963 was withdrawn.

A visitor to Quainton Road will also find numerous coaches of interest. Beyond the display area on the 'up' side can be found a three-coach set of London Transport CO/CP stock of 1938 vintage, used on the surface and sub-surface lines of the Underground until the early 1980s. The coach at the Aylesbury end, no 542433, is the remains of two trains partially destroyed in an air raid on Neasden Depot, 18th September 1940. Since vehicles could not be easily replaced during the war, it was decided to join the two together, and the rebuilt car entered service in September 1941, remaining thus until February 1981.

In the main restoration shed can be found numerous vintage vehicles restored to a very fine standard. One of these is London, Chatham & Dover Railway (LCDR) 1st class no 9, built c1880 at the Longhedge, Battersea, works of the LCDR. In the 1920s it was sold to Woolwich Arsenal for use on an internal railway system and when Quainton Road acquired it in 1962 it cost a mere £7!

The Buckinghamshire Railway Centre is continually seeing improvements. One of these is the relocation of the former LNWR Oxford Rewley Road station at Quainton Road. Dating from 1851 this grade II listed building is being rebuilt to become a visitor centre. There are hopes too that Quainton Road may become a base for main line steam operations if it succeeds with plans for a Railtrack connection. At present the centre is split in two by the Aylesbury-Calvert freight-only running and such a connection would allow rail access to the northern side of the complex as well as their ability to run shuttle services to Aylesbury and beyond whenever paths are available.

6
A Tramway Built For A Duke

Quainton Road to Brill

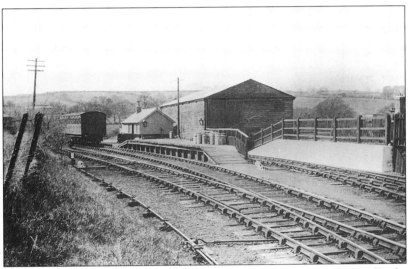

Brill station, the tramway's terminus, c1910. The line opened initially for freight but commenced passenger services in January 1872 following pressure from Brill residents. (Lens of Sutton)

The Wotton Tramway originated in the early 1870s to serve an estate of the Duke of Buckingham. Following completion of the A&BR's line from Aylesbury to Quainton Road in September 1868, work to build the tramway began. No Act of Parliament was needed since the majority of the track was laid on the Duke's land. The initial line was just under 4 miles long with goods

73

The engine shed at Brill housing two Manning Wardle locomotives circa 1903. Brill station has been completely demolished but nearby the past is recalled by 'Tramway Farm'. (Lens of Sutton)

traffic reaching Wotton on 1st April 1871. The track was standard gauge and, because it was primarily intended as a horse tramway, longitudinal sleepers were used.

By November of that year the line was extended to a brickworks near Brill and a horse-worked 1½ mile spur, known as the Kingswood branch, was built to a coal wharf at Moate Farm on Kingswood Lane. There was criticism over the location of the wharf, which was sited on low ground liable to flooding. It is said that the precise spot was chosen during an argument between the Duke and a surveyor. According to a local story, the Duke threw his hat and where it fell the wharf was built!

In January 1872 the company gave way to the folk of Brill who had been clamouring for a passenger service. A 6 hp four-wheeled steam engine was purchased from Aveling & Porter of Rochester in Kent at a cost of £400 and a Great Western composite coach was borrowed. The engine had a running speed

Metropolitan 4-4-0T locomotive no 41 awaits departure at Quainton Road in the early 1930s. Five trains ran each way on weekdays and the journey took just over 30 minutes. (Lens of Sutton)

of up to 8 mph and there were soon complaints from drivers about exposure to the weather. Water for the engine came from assorted line-side ponds and streams.

During the summer of 1872 a final section to Brill was completed giving a total route length of 6¼ miles and a second engine was acquired, similar to the first. It was now possible to run three mixed trains daily with another when required. Despite the sparse population (at the time Wotton had only 220 inhabitants) the number of passengers carried was encouraging. From just over 100 in the first month, the figure rose to 224 during April 1872.

Times were hard for the staff. Rules laid down that each servant must 'devote himself exclusively to the service, attend regularly during the appointed hours and to refrain from using improper language, cursing or swearing...'. The driver commu-

This wooden building at Quainton Road was the shelter for passengers waiting for trains to Brill. (Author)

nicated with the guard by using his engine whistle. One short blast instructed the guard to apply the brakes, two meant release the brakes and a prolonged whistle was to draw the attention of roadmen on the line or at a station. Three prolonged blasts meant trouble, perhaps a fire on the train, a derailment or possibly a fire on adjacent land amongst crops.

In 1876/7 the company spent £1,240 with Bagnells of Stafford on saddle tank locomotives designed for use on light railways or tramways and named them *Buckingham* and *Wotton*. When the Duke of Buckingham died on 26th March 1889, interest in the tramway was passed on to his nephew, Mr Gore Langton, Earl Temple. Little changed over the next year or so – new locomotives were hired but there were frequent derailments. During a hot summer in 1893 there was a water shortage for the engines. To remedy this a 1,000 gallon water tank was built to supplement the supply.

When the Oxford & Aylesbury Tramroad Company (O&AT)

Brill no 1 arrives at Quainton Road with a mixed passenger and freight set. The Brill Tramway closed in November 1935 after 60 years service. (Lens of Sutton)

took over the running in 1894, a new permanent way was constructed and stations were built. *Huddersfield*, a Manning Wardle 0-6-0 saddle tank, was bought and a similar locomotive was purchased later in the year, bearing the name *Earl Temple* in 3¾-inch letters on a brass plate. The tramway worked on the basis of 'one engine in steam' or two or more coupled together. Stations existed at Quainton Road, Waddesdon Road, Westcott, Wotton, Wood Siding (a simple waiting room only) and Brill, constructed with low platforms to suit the carriages. In 1896 Quainton Road station was resited when a bay platform was provided for Brill branch trains.

In December 1899 the Metropolitan Railway acquired the lease of the tramway with an option to purchase, an option that was never taken up. The Metropolitan continued to work the line using Wotton no 2 (purchased in February 1899) and Brill no 1 (previously named *Earl Temple*). *Huddersfield* was found to be in

A class A 4-4-0T Beyer Peacock locomotive approaches Westcott station on the Brill branch. This engine was formerly used on the Metropolitan line but it became redundant with electrification. (Lens of Sutton)

poor condition and was sold for a low sum. The coach used was a 3rd class rigid-eight-wheeler previously hired by the O&AT from the Metropolitan Railway, since the original coach had become 'a little out of condition'. The Metropolitan coach had its gas fittings replaced by oil lamps and at Quainton Road the bay platform was modified to accommodate it.

Wotton no 2 failed in March 1903 and a Sharp Stewart 2-4-0T class D engine was acquired. The track in the Brill yard was already in a poor condition but the new locomotive damaged it further and it needed replacing in August 1903 at a cost of £804. Derailments along the branch had become so frequent that the Metropolitan introduced D class engines nos 71 and 72 from its Verney Junction-Aylesbury line and sold its two Manning Wardle engines, Brill no 1 and Wotton no 2, to contractors.

With the Metropolitan tracks through Quainton Road forming part of the Great Central route to the North, it was logical that the two companies should combine. In August 1905 Parliament passed the Metropolitan & Great Central Railway Companies

The original station building at Westcott stands in the garden of privately owned 'Station House'. (Author)

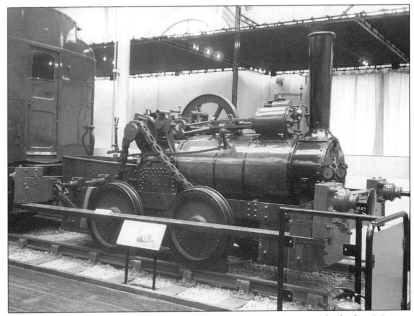

One of the Aveling & Porter engines, no 807, that worked the Wotton Tramway can be found today at the London Transport Museum at Covent Garden. (Author)

Act, thus establishing the Met & G C Joint Committee (M&GC jt). A section in the Act included the Wotton Tramway, whereby the Joint Committee assumed the lease on the same date although final agreement was not reached until 11th June 1913.

Meantime under provisions in an Act of 1899, the Great Western & Great Central Joint Committee had received approval to build a railway which would pass over the tramway, giving Wotton a second station. When this line opened in April 1906, the tramway lost many of its passengers with an alternative and fast route now available to London.

The condition of the tramway track continued to cause concern and the M&GC jt were compelled to relay it. When completed the Board of Trade agreed that the speed limit could be raised to 25 mph although certain restrictions remained such as over level crossings where an 8 mph limit was maintained. With electrification coming to the Metropolitan's Underground lines, two redundant steam locomotives found their way to the tramway. These were class A 4-4-0T Beyer Peacock engines nos 23 and 41, and they took the place of the earlier D class engines.

The O&AT tried to sell the line but the M&GC jt was not interested since it was content to continue the leasing arrangement. In 1923 the O&AT had the line valued at £34,730. An approach was made to the GWR to purchase the tramway but after several months it decided against. Other moves proved equally futile and little further transpired until 1933 when the London Passenger Transport Board (LPTB) was formed, and the Metropolitan Railway and the District Railway came under one ownership. In 1935 the LPTB decided it was not prepared to continue suburban services to Aylesbury and beyond. The tramway (now known as the Brill branch) was to close.

The last train ran on 30th November 1935. *The Times* of 2nd December 1935 reported, 'For the last time an antiquated little tank engine drew an equally antiquated passenger coach along the line between Quainton Road and Brill. It stopped at each of the five stations on the line. Documents, records and all valuables from each station were placed in the guards van and then the station lights were put out and the train steamed along to its destination at Quainton Road'. The railway, buildings and equipment were put up for sale with waiting rooms going for as little as £5 each. After over 60 years the tramway had reached a sad end.

Today the track can be traced and numerous buildings have survived. At the Buckinghamshire Railway Centre at Quainton Road the wooden waiting room on platforms 2 and 3 was once a shelter for passengers waiting for Brill trams. At Westcott the original station building has survived the years. It stands in the garden of privately owned 'Station House' and it carries LNER signs as well as a name board *Westcott*, a true copy of the original. The owners, Ian and Belinda Lodwick, have plans to restore the building to its original state and include a museum. In addition they propose to lay a section of track and acquire a Manning Wardle locomotive. Clearly the tramway is far from forgotten.

Brill station building has gone but there is one further reminder of the tramway. One of the Aveling & Porter engines, no 807, that worked the Wotton Tramway was rescued from a brickyard in 1951 by the Industrial Locomotive Society and it can be found at the London Transport Museum at Covent Garden.

7

A Branch To Newport Pagnell And A Steam Tramway

Wolverton to Newport Pagnell
The Wolverton & Stony Stratford Tramway

Wolverton station which also served a line to Newport Pagnell until the branch closed in September 1964. Wolverton was at one time the site for a railway works for the London & Birmingham Railway but when this moved to Crewe the works concentrated on carriage building. (Lens of Sutton)

Wolverton to Newport Pagnell

Parliament agreed a 4 mile single-track branch from Wolverton to Newport Pagnell on 16th June 1863. Just over two years later

Bradwell, an intermediate station on the single-line Newport Pagnell branch, photographed not long before closure. In earlier times there were difficulties when locomotives drew water at the station because it came from the town's supply, causing frequent problems for many local householders. (Lens of Sutton)

the first engine went down the line hauling 17 wagons each crammed with the navvies who had helped to build it but it was not until the following year that the railway opened for freight and cattle. Finally on 2nd September 1867 the great day came when passenger trains commenced services. The streets were decorated, church bells rang out and the Swan Hotel carried a huge illuminated star. At 1.15 pm a free trip to Wolverton was offered but so many turned up that hundreds were left behind on the platform. In the waiting room, railway officials and their friends were served with champagne.

The LNWR worked the line and staff employed included an engine driver, a fireman and three permanent way men. The driver received 42/- per week and his fireman 24/6d while permanent way men received between 17/- and 22/-. The two intermediate stations of Bradwell and Great Linford each employed one man who, in his spare time, delivered parcels within a mile of his station. Traffic was busy and the new service

Great Linford on the Newport Pagnell branch which opened to passengers on 2nd September 1867. (Lens of Sutton)

brought about the revival of the Newport Pagnell Steeplechase with special trains carrying spectators. Only one engine was allowed on the line at one time and the train became known as 'Nobby'.

There was a proposal that the branch should be extended to Olney on the Midland Railway line between Bedford and Northampton. Work began and a bridge over the Newport to Wolverton road was built. Further construction work was carried out along the route but the project was abandoned and all work stopped. In 1900 a spur was constructed close to Wolverton station to connect the branch with the up slow line. This formed an angle so that Royal Train coaches could be turned. A proposal to electrify the branch came from the LNWR in 1904. It was considered such a move would bring about considerable saving but the idea did not materialise. Locally nobody really thought there would be an electrified 'Nobby'.

During the Second World War an engine driver at Newport Pagnell decided to give the night-duty shed labourer, Joe

The terminus at Newport Pagnell prior to its closure in 1964. During the previous century work began to extend the line to Olney but the proposal was abandoned. The branch track at the terminus was lifted during 1990 and today only the sign 'Station Road' shows where the site existed. (Lens of Sutton)

Ashton, a fright by placing detonators in front of his engine. When the labourer, at 2 am, moved the engine forward to load it with coal, there was a series of successive loud bangs which echoed across the quiet countryside. At first Joe was not unduly concerned but he became very anxious when he saw, crossing the adjoining field, soldiers with rifles at the ready deployed in a pincer movement around the engine shed. The loud noise had alerted the Home Guard in their nearby headquarters!

The water supply for locomotives at Wolverton was at best no more than a trickle so drivers endeavoured to use a water column at the intermediate station of Bradwell. This water came from the town's supply and as Bradwell expanded, many of the houses at what became Top End, higher than the station, found that when the engine was taking water, they were losing their supply. On Mondays housewives often shook their fists at engine drivers when their weekly wash was interrupted. Eventually drivers were forbidden from taking water from

Bradwell on a Monday. As more houses were built so the situation got worse and in the end the column wheel was padlocked.

When proposals to close the line were announced the people of Newport Pagnell were determined to fight. An enquiry was held on 7th June 1964 but, despite many forceful arguments, it was decreed that the line should go. On 5th September 1964, ex-LMS 2-4-2T no 1222 waited with the 5.34 pm train from Newport Pagnell. Crowds watched as 'cleaners' gave 'Nobby' a final wash and brush up and accidentally emptied a bucket of water over Dr Beeching's double. Amidst cheers and long blasts on the whistle the train pulled away and at Great Linford and Bradwell many mourned its passing. For a while freight trains continued and then they went as well.

The Wolverton & Stony Stratford Tramway

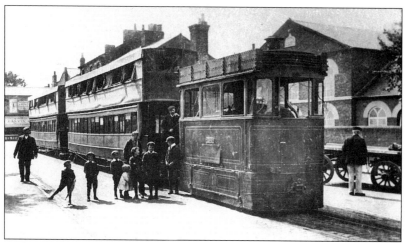

Wolverton & Stony Stratford's Green tram no 1 about to haul two 100-seater cars, c1910. The sag in the cars through heavy loads is already beginning to show. (Lens of Sutton)

87

Bagnall no 5 and a 100-seater car at the Foresters Arms awaiting departure to Wolverton. Bogies were placed at the extreme ends of the car so that the couplings remained central over the track when negotiating curves. (Lens of Sutton)

Prior to the coming of the tramway, transport between Wolverton and Stony Stratford had been sparse with only a number of small horse buses making the journey. One, owned by Mr Rich, could carry only four passengers inside and two outside. Another 'bus', owned by Joseph Clare who was landlord at the Cock Inn in the High Street, could accommodate just two inside and two outside. Only a few doors away was the Bull Inn owned by Thomas Carter and there was much rivalry between the two landlords. Both became well known for their tall stories and it has been said that this is how the expression 'a Cock and Bull story' originated.

A first attempt to build a light railway came in November 1882 but this did not prove successful. Further attempts were made over the next few years but it was not until 18th August 1886 that serious progress was made. Charles Herbert Wilkinson of

88

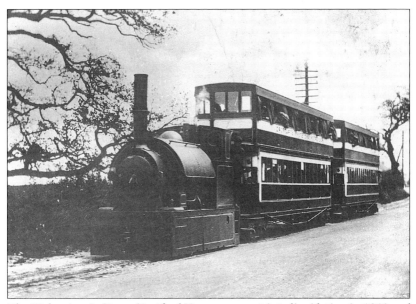

The Wolverton & Stony Stratford Tramway went into liquidation in 1919 and was taken over by the LNWR (LMS from grouping). Services were suspended during the 1926 General Strike and were never resumed. (Lens of Sutton)

Wilkinson & Co, a local firm of contractors, showed interest and he agreed a contract to build a line for £13,325. The company was known as the Wolverton, Stony Stratford & District Light Railways Co Ltd.

Board of Trade sanction for services to commence was given on 20th May 1887. The line was mostly single and it was built to the 3 ft 6 in gauge. Public passenger traffic began a week later on 27th May between the Barley Mow Inn at Stony Stratford and Wolverton railway station to connect with all up and down trains and also at times to suit local workers. Initially two steam tram-engines supplied by Krauss of Munich hauled large covered-top double-deck passenger cars obtained from the Midland Carriage and Wagon Co of Shrewsbury.

Later that year an extension of 2 miles 3 chains from Stony Stratford's High Street to Deanshanger opened. Work went ahead immediately and a line running almost parallel to the

At Milton Keynes Museum, restoration of a 44 ft long Wolverton & Stony Stratford tramcar makes excellent progress. (Author)

Grand Junction Canal opened later that year. In March 1888 a contract was agreed with the LNWR for delivery of goods from Wolverton. Despite this by mid-1889 the company ran into serious financial problems and on 4th September it declared itself insolvent and went into voluntary liquidation. This was contested by various creditors but a Court Order on 26th October closed the line. For about two years the local people had no trams and it was not until 1891 that a local benefactor, Herbert Samuel Leon of Bletchley Park, joined with the local Field family to rescue the company. After negotiations with the Receiver, a public service was reinstated on 20th November 1891. This was a purely private arrangement which lasted until September 1893 when yet another tramway company with an even longer title, the Wolverton and Stony Stratford and District New Tramway Company Limited, was formed, controlled by the Leon and Field families.

The Deanshanger extension was no longer in use and the

Stony Stratford terminus was cut back to the Cock Inn. The carriage of freight was confined mainly to LNWR parcel traffic and the handling of mail for the Postmaster General. The earlier Krauss tram-engines were replaced by engines from T. Green & Sons with the Krauss no 3 kept as stand-by.

In 1900 a further tram-engine was purchased from the Brush Electrical Company but it was hardly a satisfactory acquisition. Its cylinders were smaller than the Krauss engines and it could just about haul a workmen's tram. It continually broke down necessitating expensive and difficult repairs. To carry the workers there were three large double-deck cars, each on two 4-wheel bogies and capable of seating 100 passengers. The cars were 44 ft long and each had as many as 16 windows on either side. In later years the cars developed a visible sag in the centre because of the numbers carried and the cars had to be strengthened.

In 1910 economies and increasing motor traffic caused the High Street section to be abandoned and the trams found a new terminus outside the Foresters Arms in the Wolverton Road. Not surprisingly the presence of 44 ft long cars in formation created problems for other road vehicles. The trams received their first direct competition in 1914 when motor buses from Bedford extended their service to Stony Stratford. Relief came for the trams when war was declared and the whole of the Bedford bus fleet was requisitioned by the War Office. As the war progressed so maintenance of the tramway system became increasingly difficult. Costs outstripped revenue and in 1916 a motorbus was introduced to help maintain a regular timetable. By the end of the war in 1918 the condition of the tramway was described as 'little better than derelict'.

As a result the company went into liquidation on 17th July 1919 and matters were worsened when the local authorities refused to become involved. Since 700 workers were still being carried daily, the LNWR stepped in and at the end of 1919 purchased the entire undertaking – a move it was soon to regret. A small saddle-tank locomotive was purchased from W & G Bagnall & Co and the tramway was completely relaid with concrete placed beneath the rails. Meantime by the spring of 1920 motor buses from Bedford were providing a half-hourly service

Upstairs on the restored car, the knifeboard seats have been reconstructed to a high standard. The upper deck had no windows — tarpaulin sheets were used in bad weather. (Author)

through Stony Stratford and the trams, with their 8 mph speed limit, continued to lose money. The London, Midland & Scottish Railway Company, which took over the LNWR in 1923, struggled on with the trams now almost deserted. On 4th May 1926, during the General Strike, services were suspended never to be resumed.

Numerous items from the Wolverton & Stony Stratford Tramway can be found at the Milton Keynes Museum in Wolverton (open between Easter and the end of October, Wednesday to Sunday). Transport is a strong theme at the museum with exhibits ranging from tram tickets to relics of the original tramcars. When visited by the author in June 1999, restoration of 44 ft-long car no 2 was making excellent progress. One end of car no 2 had been used in the past as a chicken run. The other half, found at Piddington near Northampton, was in use as a garden workshop as well as a home for a model railway. Car no 2's stairs were being made in the museum but the upper doors came from the original — found as part of an allotment shed in Stony Stratford. The doors measure 4 ft 8 in by 1 ft 8 in and they must have proved a struggle for the conductor of the day, described as a 'short fat man'!

8

'Lost' LNWR Branches, A Robbery And A Narrow Gauge Railway

Cheddington to Aylesbury
'The Great Train Robbery'
Leighton Buzzard to Dunstable
The Leighton Buzzard Narrow Gauge Railway

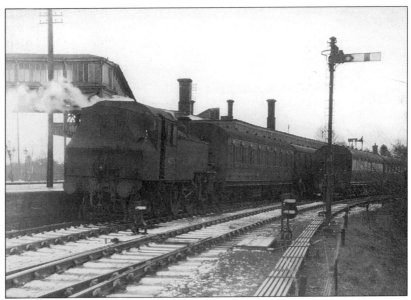

Class 2 2-6-2T no 41275 (designed by Ivatt and built at Crewe in 1950 to LMS design) with coaches waits at Cheddington on the Aylesbury branch on 31st January 1953. (John H. Meredith)

Aylesbury High Street station on 31st January 1953 on the last day of a passenger service from Cheddington. Freight services continued for a further ten years. (John H. Meredith)

Cheddington to Aylesbury

When the single-track railway from Cheddington to Aylesbury opened on 10th June 1839 three trains ran each way on weekdays and two on Sundays. All connected with London trains at Cheddington. Services were operated from the outset by locomotives and coaches from the London & Birmingham Railway (L&BR). Two small Bury 2-2-0 locomotives were used which were named *Aylesbury no 1* and *Aylesbury no 2*. The station at Aylesbury aroused much interest, Whishaw's *Railways of Great Britain & Ireland* (1842) stating, 'The station is conveniently laid. It is one of the best-arranged stations for a short line railway that we have anywhere met with'.

During the first years of its life the Aylesbury Railway's future was uncertain. Plans that it should be absorbed by rival

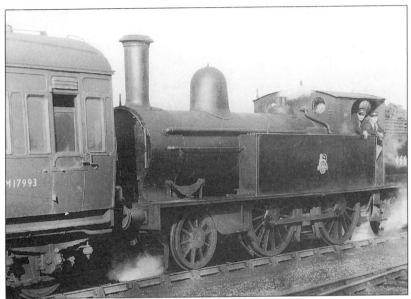

Ex-LNWR Webb 2-4-2T no 46601 (LMS class 1P) built 1890, seen at Aylesbury High Street station on 31st January 1953 awaiting departure. (John H. Meredith)

companies came to nothing as various proposals failed. Eventually the L&BR took it under an Act obtained on 16th July 1846. At the same time the L&BR became the London & North Western Railway (LNWR) which in 1851 revived an earlier plan to connect Tring with Oxford via the Aylesbury Railway and Thame. Although approved by the House of Commons, the project was rejected by the House of Lords. It had been proposed the line would cross the Aylesbury branch close to Marston Gate level crossing, where later the only intermediate station was opened. In any event, the plan was poorly received by the Aylesbury residents who were not at all happy about the prospect of a level crossing in their town's High Street.

An incident took place in 1852 which proved the usefulness of the new electric telegraph already installed on the main line. A robbery took place in Aylesbury and the thief used the branch line to make his escape. The police, knowing of his movements,

Cheddington station, June 1999. Until 1953 a branch line to Aylesbury left from a bay platform (now demolished) on the right. (Author)

made urgently for Tring station where the electric telegraph was used. When the train arrived at Euston the thief was duly arrested. The device was installed at Aylesbury station on 23rd July 1859 when the local press loudly proclaimed, 'Aylesbury is now in communication with London – indeed all the world'.

On 12th July 1883, the branch line received a Royal visit. In his book, *The Aylesbury Railway*, Bill Simpson wrote that when King Edward VII was Prince of Wales, he visited the LNWR Aylesbury station en route to Waddesdon Manor. Unfortunately the LNWR had made little effort to decorate the station although everything appeared 'in a neat and polished condition'. The townsfolk made up for any omission with a generous display of bunting, streamers and placards to welcome the Prince. Perhaps the highlight of the event was the generosity of the gas company which made available free 10,000 cu ft of gas to illuminate the decorations by night.

97

Aylesbury station greatly improved when, faced with the threat of increased competition, a more conveniently sited building opened on 16th June 1889 fronting the High Street. The Metropolitan Railway had already reached as far north as Chesham and plans were well in hand to reach Aylesbury. The new LNWR station was built in brick with its single platform under a glass canopy. The number of staff compared favourably with any station of today including a stationmaster, four porters, five clerks, three carters and two signalmen! Freight too was an important commodity and, with the Dominion Dairy close to the station, considerable quantities of the company's well known Golden Acre butter were transported along the branch. In addition barley and hops were carried to the Aylesbury Brewery, with beer later returning to Cheddington in large vats on flat wagons. The town also gained fame with its printing firm of Hazell, Watson & Viney which, apart from many other magazines, produced and exported copies of the *Reader's Digest*.

When the joint Metropolitan and GWR station opened on 1st January 1894, the LNWR branch lost much of its importance and the branch could no longer effectively compete for London traffic. During the First World War it was used to carry vast quantities of tinned foods especially for consumption by the armed forces. The English Condensed Milk Company opened in Aylesbury in 1870 to eventually become the Nestlé Company producing large amounts of condensed milk. Many will recall the station chocolate machines which carried Nestlé products.

During the 1920s the branch became part of the London, Midland & Scottish Railway (LMS). The line, like many in the area, had its share of problems during the Second World War. A bomb exploding near Marston Gate station made many reluctant to travel by rail and on another occasion the engine shed at Aylesbury was damaged by a landmine. Nationalisation came in 1948, yet the line lingered on.

Finally, on 31st January 1953, the last train pulled into Aylesbury High Street station for its journey back to Cheddington, and eager passengers scrambled across the platform in their anxiety to obtain seats. Almost before the train had come to a halt, most of the seats were taken. The driver, Victor Bunn, and his mate, W. Hodgson, obligingly posed in their cab for photographers and then it was time to go. The honour of flagging the train out went to George Thorne who had served the line for just over 40 years. As the train left the station, detonators exploded and there was a mild outburst of cheering and waving as the engine, an ex-LNWR Webb 2-4-2T no 46601, equipped with a klaxon horn, tooted its last farewell. The *Bucks Herald* wrote nostalgically of the occasion, 'The Flyer was being cast aside as one of the things we can do without in this modern age'.

The freight service survived another ten years, much of the traffic being agricultural and livestock plus business from printers Hazell, Watson & Viney. While the station building became a store used by a local wine and spirit company, freight locomotives seen along the line included Stanier class 5s and 8Fs, as well as ex-LNWR 0-8-0s and Ivatt class tank engines. The line closed completely on 2nd December 1963.

'The Great Train Robbery'

The main line just north of Cheddington became famous on 8th August 1963 when train robbers changed a signal to red and daringly held up the Royal Mail train running from Glasgow to London at Bridego Bridge. The thieves overpowered driver Jack Mills and co-driver David Whitby, also GPO sorter Frank Dewhurst and then stole 120 bags containing some £2,600,000. The bags were loaded into waiting transport below the bridge and taken to Leatherslade Farm, near Oakley. The robbery was described as the 'most daring crime of the 20th century'.

The men responsible were relentlessly tracked down by Scotland Yard Detective Tommy Butler and eventually caught. Altogether they received 573 years in jail. Even the solicitor, John Wheater, who was found guilty of negotiating the purchase of Leatherslade Farm was sent down for three years. Only one robber, Ronald Biggs, got away. After being sentenced to 30 years in prison, he escaped to eventually settle in a villa in Rio de Janeiro in Brazil.

Bridego Bridge, near Cheddington, May 1991, where 28 years previously 'The Great Train Robbery' took place. (Author)

'The Great Train Robbery' achieved considerable publicity. One may wonder if the robbers considered the hold-up really worth while. Train driver Jack Mills, who was brutally beaten, suffered ill health for years and died in 1970. The co-driver, David Whitby, whose life was threatened, perpetually carried a knife with him until he, too, died at the age of 34. It would seem the only people to really profit were those who made a film of the episode, shot in 1967. When completed it was expected to gross over £8,000,000.

Leighton Buzzard to Dunstable

The Dunstable Railway from Leighton Buzzard was worked throughout much of its life by the LNWR. It was agreed by an Act of 1845 and opened for goods traffic on 29th May 1848.

Leighton Buzzard station, June 1999, on the busy Watford to Bletchley main line. Dunstable trains left from a bay platform (now demolished) with seven trains each way daily. (Author)

Passenger services followed on 1st June 1848, the first to reach Dunstable and ten years prior to the arrival of trains from Luton. The 7 mile branch was double track and its only intermediate station was at Stanbridgeford which opened to passengers in 1849 although the platforms were not completed until 1860. Leighton Buzzard station (known as Leighton until 1911) had opened in April 1838 during Stephenson's push northwards to link London and Birmingham. Earlier the London & Birmingham Railway (LNWR from 1846) had intended to build a loop line to link Leighton Buzzard with Dunstable, an area of local importance but this had not come about.

When the Leighton Buzzard to Dunstable line opened there were seven trains daily in each direction. There were no Sunday services because of a restriction imposed by a landowner over whose land much of the branch ran. Freight traffic was

Dunstable's LNWR station (Dunstable North from 1950). The locomotive appears to be ex-LNWR 0-6-2T with a push-pull train c1930. (Lens of Sutton)

comparatively light although there were useful quantities of coal delivered to Dunstable Gas Works and chalk was collected from Tottenhoe. Stanbridgeford goods traffic was mainly cattle although a market gardener from Eaton Bray sent strawberries and carnations by rail. At Leighton Buzzard there was much activity at Grovebury Sidings where sand was brought in from the nearby sandpits.

The Leighton Buzzard to Dunstable line failed to attract any important traffic. Yet excursions were many, including regular football specials for Luton Town's home matches. The 1950s and early 1960s saw the familiar decline in passenger traffic and notice was given that the passenger service would close on 30th June 1962. Since the early 1950s Ivatt 2-6-2Ts had been in use on the branch and it was one of these, no 41222, which hauled the last train, a push-pull with two well-filled coaches.

The days of the 'Dunstable Dasher' had come to an end.

Both Dunstable stations have been subsequently demolished. The site of the former LNWR-Dunstable North is used today by new offices for the South Bedfordshire District Council. At Stanbridgeford, the station building has survived as a private residence and the platform area is part of the garden. Although attractively restyled, it remains as a reminder of a 'lost line' and carries the name Stanbridgeford House.

The Leighton Buzzard Narrow Gauge Railway

The 2-ft gauge Leighton Buzzard Railway was built in 1919 to

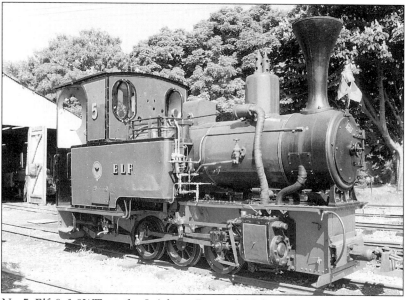

No 5 Elf 0-6-0WT at the Leighton Buzzard Light Railway, equipped with large firebox and spark arresting chimney for wood burning. The engine was built originally for the Likomba Banana Co, at Cameroon, West Africa. (Edwin Lambert)

Locomotive no 1, Chaloner, an 0-4-0VBT, on the Leighton Buzzard Light Railway dates back to 1877. (Edwin Lambert)

convey high quality sand over a 3-mile line from quarries to main railway sidings at Leighton Buzzard. Its best years were in the 1930s and again during the Second World War when sand once again increased in importance and petrol was scarce. In his book, *The Leighton Buzzard Light Railway*, S. A. Leleux wrote that during the war all sign posts, place names etc were removed to avoid helping any invading army. The company plate therefore became 'Light Railway Company Limited' and it was said that during this time at least one rail enthusiast arrived not knowing where he was!

Early in 1969 it seemed an end was close when British Rail announced it intended to close its Leighton Buzzard Billington Road and Grovebury sidings. This meant that the narrow gauge railway had lost its link with the standard gauge tracks. Application was made by the quarry owners to the County

0-4-0ST Pixie, built in 1922, photographed at Leighton Buzzard in September 1998. (Edwin Lambert)

Council for permission to use lorries, a death-blow to the railway.

Salvation of the line came when taken over by a preservation society, today forming the popular Leighton Buzzard Narrow Gauge Railway. Numerous steam locomotives have been restored and work continues on many more. The locomotives originate from various locations around the world including Spain, West Africa and even as far as India. The oldest dates back to 1877, being *Chaloner*, an 0-4-0VBT which is believed was first used at slate quarries in Wales. There are also numerous operational diesels plus large quantities of rolling stock. Considerable hard work by members has resulted in the restoration of many locomotives. In addition members have built the majority of the coaches as well as the platforms and station buildings. The railway is well worth a visit. It is run by a society where enthusiasm and dedication can be clearly seen.

105

9

'Great Northern' Branches Across Two Counties

Hertford to Hatfield
Hatfield to Dunstable
Hatfield to St Albans

Hatfield on the King's Cross/Hitchin/Peterborough line. In steam days this was a busy junction where it was possible to catch trains to St Albans, Luton and Hertford. (Lens of Sutton)

Hertford's GNR station at Cowbridge which closed to passengers on 2nd June 1924. When the Hertford Loop line opened, passengers used the new Hertford North station. (Lens of Sutton)

Hertford to Hatfield

Rail services between Hertford and Hatfield began on 1st March 1858 over a 9 mile branch with intermediate stations at Hertingfordbury and Cole Green. It began as the Hertford & Welwyn Junction Railway but, after company changes, it became part of the GNR in 1861. Locomotives and rolling stock were provided by the GNR and in Hertford a station was opened at Cowbridge, about half a mile west of the GER Hertford East station. Five trains ran each way daily with two on Sundays. Since trains from Hertford were not allowed to cross the main Kings Cross to Peterborough line at Welwyn, the branch was taken southwards to terminate at Hatfield. There was no station at Welwyn and it was not until 1920 that the Hertford branch provided a crude platform where trains stopped by request. It was to be another six years before a more substantial station was built, from which beginnings came the vast industrial area of

107

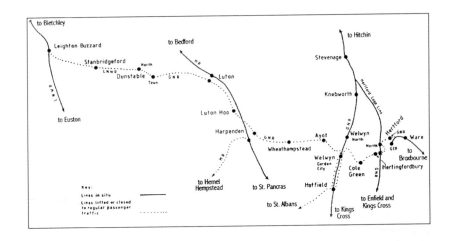

Class A4 4-6-2 no 4492 'Dominion of New Zealand' emerges from Welwyn tunnel in 1937 on the main LNER route northwards to Peterborough and Grantham. (Barry Hoper)

Hertingfordbury on the GNR Hertford to Hatfield branch which closed in June 1951. Freight services survived another 11 years until 1962. (Lens of Sutton)

Welwyn Garden City. The first factory to be built was that of the Shredded Wheat Company which developed a daily run of up to 30 wagons a day. Another pioneer of the time was Frank Murphy who in 1930 with three men founded a wireless factory. Within three years there was an output of 600 radios daily.

The branch's Hertford station at Cowbridge became redundant when a loop line was built from Stevenage to Enfield, providing a station at Hertford North. The loop came into existence because the GNR was experiencing serious bottleneck problems on its main line into King's Cross. Rather than bear the costs to widen track and enlarge tunnels on its main line, the GNR gained Parliamentary approval in 1898 to complete this 'bypass'. Progress was very slow. It was not completed until 1920 and passenger services did not commence until 2nd June 1924. The Cowbridge station closed to passengers on the same day and branch trains used the new Hertford North station. The route to Cowbridge with a connection through to the Hertford East GER station was kept open for freight.

During the 1939-1945 war, the line from Hertford to Hatfield was connected with the up main line at Welwyn and from September 1944 Hertford trains terminated at Welwyn Garden City instead of Hatfield. Passenger services continued until 18th June 1951 when the branch became an early victim to closure. The last train, hauled by class N7 locomotive no 69695, carried many passengers and reached Welwyn Garden City at 7.33 pm. In a last moment of glory, two weeks before closure, an LMS-reconstructed Liverpool & Manchester engine and three coaches were used to help make the Anna Neagle film *Lady with the Lamp*.

Hatfield to Dunstable

At 10.33 am on 26th July 1948 a porter spotted a fire at Ayot station (between Wheathampstead and Welwyn) just after a train had left. Two hours later the station was gutted and the track had curled and buckled in the heat. Spectators helped the firemen handle a pump and hoses over the burning track and across fields to a nearby pond. Services were restored during the afternoon but the station was never rebuilt and subsequently closed to passenger traffic on 26th September 1949.

The branch began as the Luton, Dunstable & Welwyn Junction Railway which obtained Parliamentary approval on 16th July 1855. After opening a passenger service between Dunstable and Luton on 3rd May 1858, the company found itself short of funds so the extension beyond Luton was shelved. It was only when the amalgamation with the Hertford & Welwyn Railway took place to form the Hertford, Luton & Dunstable Railway (HL&DR), that further construction could be considered. Even then the work was not carried out on time and a further Act of 21st July 1859 had to be issued to allow completion. A line between Luton and Welwyn eventually opened on 1st September 1860 with intermediate stations at New Mill End (Luton Hoo from 1891), Harpenden, Wheathampstead

110

Dunstable's former GNR Church Street station (renamed Dunstable Town in 1927), c1910. The station closed to passengers in April 1965 and the site has been subsequently demolished. (Lens of Sutton)

and Ayott St Peter's (Ayot from 1878). Like the Hertford to Hatfield branch, HL&DR trains could not cross the GNR main line at Welwyn so trains had to continue to Hatfield. The single-track section of just over 20 miles between Luton and Dunstable was initially worked by the London & North Western Railway (LNWR) but when Hatfield was reached, the GNR took over the whole line.

When services began in 1858 between Dunstable (Dunstable Town from 1927) and Luton there were five trains each way daily and from 1860 services began between Luton and Hatfield. On weekdays two trains later went on through to Leighton Buzzard. Passenger traffic increased satisfactorily over the years that followed. Even though the Midland Railway (MR) had reached Luton offering a more direct route to and from London, it did not always offer a better service. Many MR trains stopped

111

Dunstable Town station shortly before closure. From the early 1950s Ivatt 2-6-2Ts were much in use on the branch. The trains were nicknamed 'Dunstable Dashers'. (Lens of Sutton)

at all stations so passengers often chose express trains from Hatfield to King's Cross, with certain trains providing a through service from Dunstable. It was suggested that one particular train, the 7 pm to Hatfield, was reliably punctual since it frequently carried the Prime Minister, Lord Salisbury.

Luton, being the largest town on the route, became an important freight centre with a large coal yard built in 1906 to the south of Luton Bute Street station. Luton was also the centre of the hat industry with many consignments received and despatched by rail. Wheathampstead also carried its share of goods traffic. Being an agricultural area, the railway was used for transporting animals and local nurseries despatched large quantities of fresh salad. A commodity often imported into the station yard was manure from the London Zoo although residents in Rose Lane opposite the sidings were not so happy about this.

Smallford station (page 114) on the branch from Hatfield to St Albans was originally known as Springfield. It was renamed Smallford in 1879. The platform building became an office to a scrap metal yard. (Lens of Sutton)

By the 1930s traffic declined with passengers lost to good local bus services but freight remained active for a number of years. Luton prospered when the Vauxhall motor industry came to the town, but when it stopped sending export vehicles by rail, branch freight declined. Following the abolition of steam working, three-unit Metro-Cammell railcars took over much of the passenger working. When closure of the line was threatened for 6th January 1965 under the 'Beeching Axe', there were many objections and a reprieve was obtained. Unhappily it was only a brief one and the line finally closed to passengers on 26th April 1965. The last train carrying a nameplate 'The Last Skimpot Flyer' (the nickname Skimpot referred to a farm along the route) was hauled by a diesel type 1 no D8046.

Although the track between Welwyn and Luton was later ripped up, the single line between Luton and Dunstable has remained in existence. Over the years speculation has continued over the possibility of restoring a public transport service

113

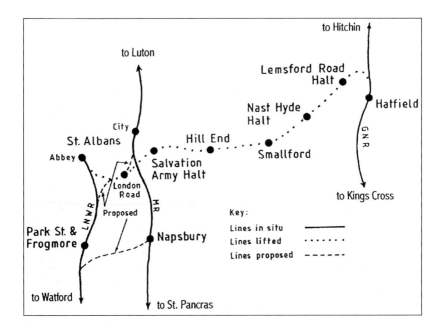

although no firm decision has been made. Transport chiefs have considered conversion of the disused line into a bus-only road while another view put forward envisaged a rail link to include Luton Airport. A final decision has still to be made, a factor very much dependent upon the availability of finance.

Hatfield to St Albans

Parliamentary approval for a line to be built from St Albans to Hatfield was granted on 30th June 1862. There was difficulty in raising finance but, with GNR support, the Hatfield & St Albans Railway Company went ahead with construction of the line. The line opened on 16th October 1865 with one intermediate station planned at Springfield (renamed Smallford in 1879) although this was not ready in time for the line's opening.

The Act gave the GNR (which worked the line) running

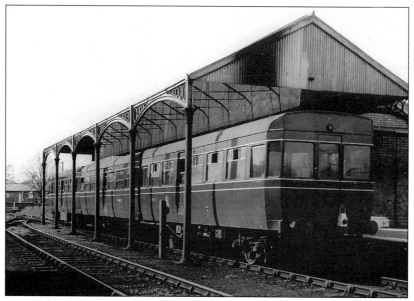

A British United Traction 3-car multiple unit set at St Albans Abbey, used on the Watford branch in the 1950s. These cars were disliked by many passengers who complained of 'rough riding and ineffective heating' so the line reverted to steam during the winter 1955/56. (Lens of Sutton)

powers into the LNWR's St Albans station which had opened earlier in 1858 as terminus for a line from Watford. Passenger coaches were four-wheeled vehicles, lit by oil lamps, and it was not until 1883 that gas-lit coaches were introduced. The coaches were probably hauled by Sharp 2-2-2Ts, and the branch journey took 15 minutes. The single fare from St Albans to King's Cross was 3/6d first class, 2/6d second class and 1/11½d third class. If a passenger took a horse with him it cost an extra 5/- and a dog 1/-. On weekdays, trains went through to the LNWR (Abbey) station but on Sundays the two passenger trains terminated at the GNR St Albans London Road station.

When a MR (later LMS) main line opened through St Albans, receipts on the GNR branch fell and debts could not be paid. In 1870 a Receiver was appointed and the independent company had little choice but to become totally absorbed by the GNR. This

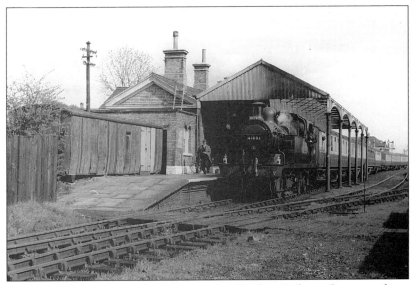

Ex-LMS 0-4-4T Stanier class 2P no 41901 heads a Railway Correspondence & Travel Society tour on 27th April 1958 reaching St Albans from Watford. (Lens of Sutton)

was formalised by an Act of Parliament on 1st November 1883. Debts were paid off, shareholders received 23% of the face value of their shares and the Hatfield & St Albans Railway Company no longer existed. The branch continued under its new owner-ship although hopes to build up London traffic were frustrated by the MR's new line, with the GNR continuing to run at a loss. To encourage traffic a few through coaches ran from St Albans to King's Cross but these did not survive long. Cheap excursions were arranged which included a holiday of up to six days in Scarborough for a return rail fare of 7/6d. Similarly passengers could travel to King's Cross in 1893 for 1/9d third class return to attend such outings as a Brewery Exhibition at the Royal Agricultural Hall, 'Niagara Falls in Winter' at Westminster or a Dog Show at the Crystal Palace. The last visit required a further 1/6d which also included admission to the show.

In 1899 a further intermediate station opened at Hill End (to serve the Herts County Mental Hospital), followed by Salvation

London Road station at St Albans closed to passenger traffic in October 1951. (Lens of Sutton)

Army Halt where a printing works opened in 1901. The press published such books as *The War Cry* and *Young Soldier*. Nast Hyde Halt followed in 1910. By the late 1930s the number of passengers was declining and when the war came in 1939 the LNER (formerly GNR) withdrew all passenger services. Within three months trains had to restart to meet the needs of the many St Albans people travelling to the De Havilland Aircraft Works at Hatfield. After the war, numbers fell again and on 1st October 1951 the line closed to passengers for good.

The line lingered on into the 1960s with freight traffic serving the many industrial sidings along the branch, during which time special excursions were organised by various societies. The branch saw fame too when stations were used for a number of film and TV productions. Smallford station was used more than once and, more recently, London Road station was used for TV films such as *The Return of the Saint* and *The Rivals of Sherlock Holmes*. London Road station today is a listed building and much of the old trackbed has become a walk/cycle path.

When the author visited St Albans by car, he was stopped

outside the town with other traffic at a police survey and asked various questions. The officer asked finally, 'Where are you going?' Back came the answer, 'London Road railway station'. 'But that's been closed for years ...', he was replying as the car pulled away. The officer could still be seen in the car rear-view mirror scratching his head.

10

The 'Nicky Line' To Harpenden

Hemel Hempstead to Harpenden

Hemel Hempstead station, c1910. The single line branch of almost 9 miles to Harpenden opened for passenger traffic on 16th July 1877. (Lens of Sutton)

The line that began as the Hemel Hempstead Railway was unique since it was the only Midland Railway branch in Hertfordshire. It began as a link between Hemel Hempstead (originally spelt Hemel Hempsted) town and the LNWR Boxmoor station to the west. Boxmoor (today's main line Hemel Hempstead station) was remote from the town and the Hemel Hempstead Railway succeeded in obtaining Parliamentary approval in 1863 to build a connecting line across Boxmoor

119

Hemel Hempstead, June 1999, on the main Euston to Birmingham line. Until 1912 the station was known as Boxmoor. The station closed to freight in 1966. (Author)

Common to the LNWR goods yard. It had been intended that it would be used by passenger traffic as well as goods but, when constructed, the only physical link with the LNWR was by turntable. The short section was little used probably because of difficulties with the Boxmoor Trust, wealthy owners of the protected common known as Boxmoor, although some freight traffic did later develop.

Construction of a line from Hemel Hempstead to Harpenden began in 1866 but it was not completed until 16th July 1877. On the first day, there were free first-day rides for everyone. Many considered the line was charmingly eccentric, sometimes operated with a loaned 4-4-0T locomotive pulling a rather elderly first class Pullman car available with third class fares. Hemel Hempstead was an important source of raw material from reed beds for the straw hat industry and its links at that

120

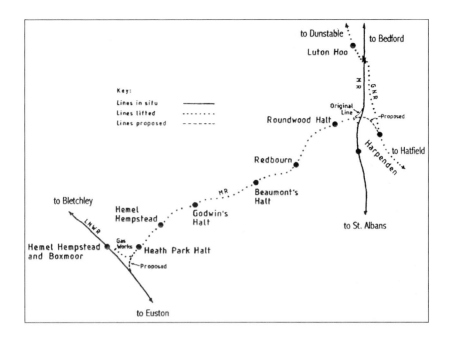

time were therefore greater with Luton than with London. There were three trains each way daily and the total journey of 13¼ miles between Hemel Hempstead and Luton took about 40 minutes.

The Hemel Hempstead Railway's connection with the main MR line at Harpenden gave passengers access to St Pancras trains, this causing much friction with the LNWR and its main line service to Euston. By the 1880s relations had deteriorated to the extent that on one occasion a Midland Railway locomotive which penetrated the LNWR yard at Boxmoor was held back by force by the removal of rails in its path. It was inevitable that Hemel Hempstead Railway traffic should suffer with London-bound passengers from Hemel Hempstead finding it quicker to travel via Boxmoor, reaching the station by an LNWR horse-bus.

The link to MR tracks at Harpenden was north-facing towards Luton. Consideration was given to a south-facing link but it was not until 1888, two years after absorption of the company by the Midland Railway, that this was completed. The original north-

121

Heath Park halt was the closest passenger trains ever got to the former LNWR Euston main line at Boxmoor. From 1905 it had the distinction of serving as a terminus on the Hemel Hempstead to Harpenden branch. (Lens of Sutton)

facing route was abandoned and trains now ran into a small bay at Harpenden beside the down fast platform. Following the Midland Railway take-over, services were increased to seven trains each way daily (with no Sunday service) with connections for St Pancras reaching London in a little more than one hour. The earliest locomotives to work the line were three George England 2-4-0 tender engines transferred from the Somerset & Dorset Joint Railway, with the numbers 9, 10 and 13 becoming 1397, 1398 and 1399. Near the Harpenden end of the line there was a steep incline of 1 in 37 which sometimes proved too much for overloaded engines and meant that loads had to be strictly limited.

In 1905 the Midland introduced a rail-motor push-pull service and it was shortly afterwards that an ex-Eastern & Midlands Railway 4-4-0T and an elderly Pullman parlour coach were introduced. After this the line was generally operated by 0-4-4T

The site of Heath Park halt in June 1999, almost 55 years after the line closed to passengers. Boxmoor House on the left has become an Arts Centre while Heath Park Hotel has been rebuilt. In the background can be determined the Kodak Hemel Hempstead centre. (Author)

and 0-6-0T engines. At first the only intermediate branch station was at Redbourn but on 9th August 1906 trains were extended from Hemel Hempstead to Heath Park halt, making the branch one of the very few to have a halt for a terminus. On the same day, to encourage local traffic, Beaumont halt and Godwin halt were opened and the service was further increased to nine trips daily. Roundwood halt came later on 8th August 1927.

The Hemel Hempstead branch became part of the London, Midland & Scottish Railway (LMS) in 1923 which introduced an alternative bus service in 1929. This reduced train services to peak times only so that just one locomotive was needed. The buses connected Hemel Hempstead and Boxmoor and rail tickets could be used.

A reduced service survived the Second World War but

Harpenden station in LMS days. The locomotive in the foreground is a Fowler 2-6-4T class 3P. A journey on the 9 mile 'Nicky' branch to Hemel Hempstead took just under half an hour. (Lens of Sutton)

passenger trains finally ceased on 16th June 1947 during a coal crisis. After closure rail enthusiasts had an opportunity to travel the branch when on 10th August 1958 a Railway Correspondence & Travel Society tour hauled by 3F 0-6-0 no 43245 covered the tracks. In 1959 a rail link finally became available between the former LNWR goods yard and the Boxmoor Gasworks. This lasted only a few months with production of coal gas coming to an end. In July 1964 BR terminated freight traffic over the Harpenden end of the branch and in 1972 the track to Boxmoor Gasworks was removed.

By the 1980s much of the branch trackbed became a walkway, known appropriately as the 'Nicky Walk'. A number of the diesel locomotives that had served the branch survived. D2207 0-6-0DM class 04 built in 1953 went to the North Yorkshire Moors Railway and D2203 0-6-0DM, built in 1952 and used at the Hemel Hempstead Concrete Company, can be found at the Embsay & Bolton Abbey Steam Railway.

124

The down platform at Harpenden on the Thameslink line in May 1991. The bay platform that served Hemel Hempstead trains has long since gone. The original Midland platform building was destroyed by fire in the early 1970s with today's rebuilt to the same style. (Author)

Although passenger services ceased well over 50 years ago, the line is still recalled with affection by many. Some residents remember that the branch's reputation for punctuality was such that 'watches and clocks could be set by the train'. It was claimed the train became so reliable that some called her 'Faithful Annie'. Yet to those who today think they still hear the whistle of a steam engine near Hemel Hempstead's town centre, it has become 'The Ghost of Puffing Annie'.

125

11
A GER Branch To Buntingford

St Margarets to Buntingford

Hertford East station, built in 1888, seen here in the 1960s with its imposing entrance and highly decorated building. The Hertford East branch, which opened in 1843, today provides a regular commuter service. (Author)

The first sod of the Ware, Hadham & Buntingford Railway (WH&BR) was cut on 20th July 1859 between Buntingford and Westmill. In his book, *The Buntingford Branch*, P. Paye wrote that after the ceremony all present went to a large marquee erected in a nearby field where a cold lunch was served. Children were catered for separately, receiving large amounts of plum cake and

126

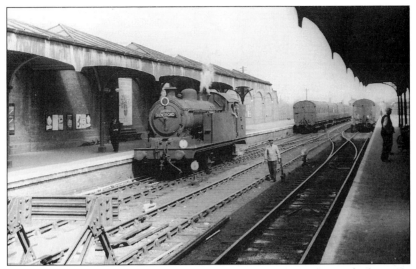

A class N7 0-6-2T locomotive runs round a passenger set at Hertford East in the early 1960s. The line was later electrified as part of a North London scheme. (Lens of Sutton)

ginger beer, and the navvies were supplied with beer in a smaller tent nearby. Unfortunately the good weather quickly gave way to torrential rain and gale force winds, and water was soon penetrating the large marquee, soaking tables, chairs and occupants alike. Some found shelter in the smaller tent but others were not so lucky.

It was intended that the branch should make its junction with the Great Eastern Railway line at Ware but instead it joined the GER tracks further south at St Margarets to avoid upsetting a landowner. The GER line between Broxbourne and Hertford had opened earlier in 1843. Unusually this 7 mile single line branch had been built to a 5 ft gauge but it was converted to standard gauge the following year.

The 13¼ mile branch from St Margarets to Buntingford opened eventually on 3rd July 1863. There had been financial problems and the bridge at Braughing gave problems even before opening. Had the ECR (which formed part of the GER from 1862) not intervened, the line could well have failed before it began.

127

A deserted Hertford East station in GER days. The branch joins the main Cambridge line at Broxbourne junction. (Lens of Sutton)

Intermediate stations were mostly wooden structures to begin with, at Mardock, Widford, Hadham, Standon, Braughing and Westmill. The line was single with passing loops and from the outset it was worked by the GER. Initially there were four trains each way daily with two on Sundays. The time for the journey from St Margarets to Buntingford was around 50 minutes but after the first few weeks this improved to 40 minutes. During the first half year almost 30,000 passengers travelled the line but goods traffic was considered disappointing. This was largely due to the fact that initially there were no goods sheds or sidings!

As time passed, relations between the WH&BR and the GER worsened. The independent branch was dissatisfied with the facilities offered by the GER, which considered its share of receipts inadequate to pay for the cost of working the line. In consequence, the GER purchased the line on 1st September 1868, just five years after the branch had opened. Problems followed and there was a derailment at Buntingford. At Westmill, a bridge constructed by an Ely contractor rotted because it had been built with low-grade timber. Track improvements were carried out

128

The former GER Ware station on the Hertford East branch. It was originally planned that the Buntingford branch would leave the Hertford line at Ware but certain landowners objected and the proposal was dropped and St Margarets chosen instead. (Lens of Sutton)

and certain stations were rebuilt after which time conditions steadily improved. Freight traffic also improved with two trains daily, one to and from Broxbourne and the other to and from Hertford.

During 1890 Braughing station, because of its remoteness, was broken into on no fewer than six occasions. The burglar was never caught but he certainly showed considerable audacity. Having gained entry to the booking office, he placed a lighted candle in the small window to examine the contents of the office at his leisure. He ripped open parcels and, on one occasion, stole the stationmaster's waistcoat, coat and gold pencil case. On another occasion he made off along the line, forced an entry into a platelayer's hut and lit a fire to cook a supper with fish stolen from a parcel!

In the summer of 1901, the first through service began when the last train of the day from Buntingford ran to Liverpool Street. By 1914 there were eleven passenger trains daily although goods

St Margarets station, c1910. A train for Buntingford awaits departure at the bay platform on the far side. (Lens of Sutton)

traffic was less encouraging. There was residential growth along the branch and from 1922 there were a number of through-coach peak-hour workings from Liverpool Street, but competition from road transport was on the increase. On 1st January 1923 the Great Eastern Railway, the Great Northern Railway and the Great Central Railway and others combined to form the London & North Eastern Railway (LNER) and various economies followed. Matters worsened on 26th January 1924 when a seven day rail strike lost the line many passengers who left the trains never to return.

During the Second World War the branch acquired an additional role when it carried war supplies to and from an ordnance depot at Buntingford. Because of the importance of the traffic, bridges were frequently guarded by members of the Home Guard. Passenger services were not badly affected and during the early part of the war trains brought evacuees from London's East End, many seeing the countryside for the first time in their lives. The branch was fortunate as far as air raids were concerned, suffering only one major incident when a stray

Staff pose at St Margarets station in early GER steam days. Trains to Buntingford used the bay on the left. During the 1920s nine trains each way served the branch. (Lens of Sutton)

V1 flying bomb exploded near the line at Hadham. Train services were suspended for two days as a result.

After the war freight traffic declined, particularly the movement of livestock during 1950 following a serious outbreak of foot and mouth disease in the Buntingford and Standon areas. The 1950s also saw a further decline in passenger traffic as private cars began to dominate. In 1959 single diesel multiple units were introduced but by the following year many off-peak trains were cancelled. Many commuters preferred to motor to a main line rather than lose time changing at St Margarets. Towards the end of its life, the branch was used for testing prototype rail vehicles intended for export. Also a number of films were made. One of these was at Hadham which adopted the name 'Upper Fringly' in the film *Postman's Knock* featuring the locomotive J15 0-6-0 no 65460.

As passenger traffic declined, so an inevitable closure date was announced. Protests were made and public meetings were held but all was in vain. Passenger closure followed from 16th

A mixed passenger-freight train hauled by ex-LNER 0-6-2T class N7 awaits departure for St Margarets from Buntingford in the early 1960s. The 13¼ mile branch failed, like so many, through competition from motor cars. (Lens of Sutton)

November 1964 with the last down train, comprising Rolls Royce/Derby railcars E51154/E59449/E50988, leaving St Margaret's bay platform at 9.45 pm on Saturday, 14th November. The driver was R. F. Hopkins and the guard W. Broad. Closure to freight traffic followed on 20th September 1965.

The former terminus at Buntingford can be found today behind the Railway Inn on the old A10 which passed through the town. It has become an office and engineering works while the platform side of the building has been lost to a housing development. Some sections of the branch trackbed have survived as footpaths but other sections have been lost following roadworks on the A10.

12
Lost 'Midland' Lines From Bedford

Bedford to Hitchin
Bedford to Northampton

Ex-Midland Railway class 2F 0-6-0 no 3707 (built 1901 to a design of S. W. Johnson) at Bedford on 10th August 1935. (Barry Hoper)

Bedford to Hitchin

Application for consent to build a line from Leicester (Wigston junction) to Bedford, with an extension to Hitchin, was first submitted by the Midland Railway in 1847 but a downturn in the

Cardington station building on the former Bedford to Hitchin line, today a privately owned and listed property. The distant signal was 'saved' from the line which closed in January 1962. (Author)

country's economy made the company pull back from such a new and costly project. In addition a war in the Crimea was threatening. In the early 1850s the landowners of Bedfordshire pressed the Midland Railway to reconsider such a proposal, with the result that the application was resubmitted and on 4th August 1853 it received Parliamentary approval. The 16¼ mile double-track stretch from Hitchin to Bedford, today no longer in existence, was part of this line.

Work eventually began late in 1853 but progress was slow and it became clear that a completion date set for October 1856 could not be met. Old Warden Tunnel was finished on time but only after numerous accidents, some fatal. Work on stations at Henlow, Shefford, Southill and Cardington was delayed because of a brick shortage and at Hitchin there was a dispute with the Great Northern Railway (GNR) where lines met. Because of a disagreement over valuation of a parcel of land, the Midland had to abandon a proposed junction at Arlesey and instead run

Not far from the former Cardington station, these massive airsheds still exist.
It was in one of these that the ill-fated R101 was housed. (Author)

alongside GNR tracks for 3 miles into Hitchin.

The branch opened on 7th May 1857 amid considerable celebrations. There were four trains each way on weekdays with freight services commencing some six months later. The fare from Hitchin to Leicester was 4/-, second class 2/- and third class 1/-. The Midland Railway claimed that it had become a London service although passengers had to change to GNR trains at Hitchin. In February 1858 the GNR allowed through Midland trains to King's Cross but charged a levy of £60,000 annually for the privilege. Meantime Midland trains were having to use the LNWR station at Bedford since plans for a joint station had not materialised. It was not until February 1859 that the Midland opened its own Bedford station on Freemen's Common, nearer to the town centre.

In 1868 the Hitchin-Bedford line lost its main-line status when the Midland opened its own line from Bedford to London. The situation had been forced by earlier problems with the GNR which objected to the number of Midland trains using its King's

Hitchin station, c1910, on the main GNR route from King's Cross to Peterborough. A footbridge across the tracks was removed pre-1914. (Lens of Sutton)

Cross sidings. In 1862 matters came to a head when the GNR summarily evicted Midland trains and the Midland saw its only future was to build an independent route. Parliamentary approval was granted in 1863 and a line via Luton and St Albans was built, reaching Moorgate Street on 13th July 1868 and St Pancras on 1st October. By 1880 the amount of traffic justified quadrupling of the track. Meantime the Hitchin-Bedford passenger services had been reduced to a shuttle service.

Plowman's Siding, between Henlow and Shefford, opened in December 1893 to accommodate wagons bringing London's household rubbish. When emptied, the wagons were filled with bricks and returned. As passenger traffic declined, so the line was converted to single except between Southill and Shefford. During the First World War a halt, Cardington Workmen's Platform, opened where in later years numerous sidings served an RAF camp.

There was further activity at Cardington in the early 1920s when the then Labour Government approved the construction of two large airships, the R100 and the R101, for Empire communication. Two vast sheds were required to house them

When staff were plentiful at Hitchin GNR, c1910. The canopy has long since been removed but the basic buildings remain the same. (Lens of Sutton)

and Cardington was to prove an ideal site. A shed already existed, built by Short Bros during 1916/17 as part of a contract to build rigid airships for the Admiralty to support the war effort. The group of nearby houses, built for employees, became known as 'Shortstown' – a name it still holds today. A second shed, built at Pulham in Norfolk, was dismantled and transported to Cardington during 1928/9.

The R100 arrived at Cardington in December 1929 from Howden in Yorkshire where it had been built and it successfully flew the Atlantic both ways. The R101, built at Cardington, underwent design changes and left for India in October 1930 without proper testing. It crashed dramatically 7½ hours into the flight near Allone in France. Following the disaster, the R100 was broken up and the airship programme terminated. It is said that the area is haunted by members of the ill-fated R101 airship crew who come back to look for their loved ones ...

When buses began services between Bedford and Hitchin in the 1920s, the railway began a slow decline from which it did not recover. Activity renewed somewhat when RAF camps were established in the area during the Second World War and

137

Southill, an intermediary station on the Midland line from Hitchin to Bedford, which closed in 1962. In its time the station boasted sidings and a cattle pen. (Author)

platforms at Henlow (renamed Henlow Camp in 1933) were extended to cope with special troop trains. By the 1950s trains comprised one carriage only and it was clear that the end was in sight. The introduction of a diesel service in 1960 did little to encourage traffic and the line closed as from 1st January 1962.

As the last train from Bedford to Hitchin prepared to pull out of Midland Road station, railway enthusiasts were there in force. Before it left, there was a cheer as Richard Lentam of the Biggleswade & District Model Railway Society placed a wreath on locomotive 2-6-2T no 84005 and, exactly on time, driver Wilf Johnson eased the train away from the platform. Before the line was finally lifted, it had one last claim to fame when a film company making *Those Magnificent Men in their Flying Machines* acquired the disused line and the tunnel.

Anyone visiting the area today can find many recollections of the past. One of these is the station building at Southill which has been tastefully converted into a private residence. The ticket

Turvey station in earlier times on the line from Bedford to Northampton. Passenger traffic was light since this was a very rural area with the station situated over a mile from Turvey village. There were five trains each way on weekdays but never any Sunday services. (Lens of Sutton)

window is still there and the platform area, sidings and cattle pen have become a garden to be proud of. Not far from Southill station and hidden among trees is an obelisk erected in 1864 as a memorial to William Henry Whitbread, as a tribute to his 'zeal and energy in promoting railways in the county'. At Old Warden the tunnel can still be found, now a nature reserve in the safe keeping of the Beds and Hunts Wildlife Trust.

Bedford to Northampton

The first attempt to build a railway between Bedford and Northampton was made in 1845 by a company known as the 'Northampton, Bedford & Cambridge Railway'. It was planned to reach Bedford at the station today known as St John's with a

Today at Turvey the platforms have gone but the attractive stone building remains to serve as an office to Cargill plc, a company of agricultural merchants. (Author)

projected line to Cambridge to follow. The plan failed to materialise and the company collapsed with shareholders having some of their investment refunded. The route was surveyed again in 1864 but, according to the *Bedfordshire Mercury*, this scheme was dropped because of huge demands made by the owners of property. It was finally an Act of 1865 that gave the go-ahead but, due to delays in securing finance plus the finding of a satisfactory contractor, further Acts had to be obtained in 1866 and 1867 to provide an extension of time.

The 21 mile line eventually opened on 10th June 1872 but due to the death of the Duke of Bedford in the same month, celebrations were delayed until 26th July, when a grand banquet was held in Bedford's Assembly Rooms and many dignitaries were present. In a speech, the chairman, Colonel Higgins, included a welcome for the many distinguished people from Northampton and, replying, the High Sheriff of Northampton spoke of the days when a horse-drawn journey from Bedford to

Northampton took three hours.

The branch left the Midland line north of Bedford at Oakley junction and there were intermediate stations at Turvey, Olney and Piddington. Like many rural stations two of them were some distance from the locality they claimed to serve. Turvey station with its attractive stone building was over a mile from its village although Olney, also in stone, was well placed in the town. Piddington was brick-built but very isolated and hard to find along a narrow country lane, with its village 2½ miles away. The branch ended at St John's Street in the middle of Northampton.

Initially there were five trains each way on weekdays but there was never any Sunday service. In January 1881 there was a severe blizzard and the evening train to Bedford became stuck in a snowdrift which had also brought down telegraph poles. F. G. Cockman wrote in the *Bedfordshire Magazine* that devotion to duty took place that night, but it was not just confined to the railway staff. Mrs Rose Sargeant, the Turvey postmistress, had taken the postbag to the station as usual that evening. She stayed there all night waiting in vain for the train to arrive and would not part with the bag until the next morning.

In 1923 the Midland Railway became part of the London, Midland & Scottish Railway (LMS) and in July 1939 it was decided to cut expenses by closing Northampton's St John's Street station. Trains were switched to the Castle station via Hardingstone junction. By this time the number of passengers was declining although specials were seen along the branch when there was horse-racing at Towcester. During the Second World War the line regained importance with well-packed trains once again. Piddington station also became busier when an Army depot opened nearby.

After the war, competition from motor transport increased and efforts were made to attract passengers. For a time diesel railcars took over from steam but they frequently broke down and steam trains were brought back. But it was too late since local folk were finding other ways to travel. Towards its end, the branch developed a very rural flavour. Track gangs snared rabbits in Ravenstone Wood and train drivers left orders, sometimes leaving coal in payment. At Olney the stationmaster was proud of his chrysanthemums in the station garden and often used

141

paper bags to protect them from the rain. They became known as 'the paper bag harvest'.

The last train hauled by an Ivatt 2-6-2T ran on 3rd March 1962, crammed with passengers. There were exploding detonators on the track and the usual wreaths were placed on the engine. Notices stuck on the windows of the two-coach push-pull read, 'Bedford-Northampton. Killed by the internal combustion engine. Farewell. RIP'. Ninety years of faithful service had come to an end.

13
LNWR Trains Towards Cambridge

The Sandy & Potton Railway and Bedford to Cambridge

Blunham, an intermediary station on the line from Bedford to Cambridge, which closed in January 1968. (Lens of Sutton)

The Sandy & Potton Railway was initially intended for goods traffic only. At a grand opening ceremony, held on 23rd June 1857, Lady Peel named one of the two engines *Shannon* after a frigate her son had commanded. The 3½ mile single-track line opened to passenger traffic on 9th November 1857 with coaches hired from the GNR. Signalling consisted of 'waving a red flag

143

when a would-be passenger from one of the farmhouses along the route wished to embark'.

Although agricultural traffic proved to be busy, passenger traffic was never outstanding, principally because the company failed to produce an extension towards Cambridge. After five years the Sandy & Potton Railway became part of the Bedford & Cambridge Railway (B&CR) which bought the line in 1862 for £20,000 to include *Shannon*. The locomotive was then resold to the contractor, Joseph Firbank, for use in constructing the new line.

The B&CR opened on 7th July 1862, worked by the LNWR from the outset. Absorbed by the LNWR in 1865, it was initially single track but as traffic grew the line was doubled between Sandy and Cambridge. The section between Bedford and Sandy remained single to avoid the expense of rebuilding river bridges. The line at Bedford (renamed Bedford St Johns in 1924) started at an end-on junction with the LNWR branch from Bletchley. Through traffic was later possible, but no arrangement followed to produce a joint station with the Midland Railway branch from Hitchin to Leicester. Strenuous efforts, supported by the Mayor of Bedford, were made in vain and passengers justifiably complained about having to walk across the town in all weathers to change trains. Between Bedford and Potton there were intermediate stations at Blunham and Sandy. Initially there were eight trains each way daily from Bedford to Cambridge with one each way on Sundays. LNWR four-wheel coaches were used with six-wheel stock being introduced around 1880.

Willington station opened on 1st May 1903 following strenuous petitioning by the villagers. Immediately prior to opening, the *Bedford Times* reported, 'At first trains will not stop except when required. Persons wishing to alight must give notice at the preceding station, and when passengers wish to join the train it will be stopped by signal'. Blunham station, a substantial building of brick construction, had two platforms plus sidings and, in addition, a longer siding leading to a linseed oil mill on the banks of the river Ivel. Between Blunham and Sandy where the A1 crossed the track, the LMSR opened a small halt in 1938 to encourage local traffic but it lasted only two years. There was no station building and tickets had to be purchased at a nearby garage.

Northbound GNR 4-4-2 locomotive no 406 with passenger train at Sandy station. The station was shared with a GNR line from Hitchin to Peterborough which crossed the Bedford branch. Quadrupling of the main GNR line has today obliterated the branch station (Lens of Sutton)

At Sandy the line from Bedford crossed the GNR line from Hitchin to Peterborough and the two companies shared the same station site. Until 1917 Sandy had two stationmasters, although an exchange siding existed between the two companies which jointly handled many tons of agricultural produce each week. Travellers on the Bedford line could enjoy their brief stop. Not only was Sandy station well known for its attractive flowerbeds and shrubs but in later years there could be an occasional glimpse of the *Flying Scotsman* thundering past on its journey between King's Cross and Edinburgh.

Potton station was substantially built with a cast-iron canopy supported by stanchions carrying intricate cast-ironwork on the 'up' platform. During its earlier days large quantities of agricultural goods, such as potatoes and onions, left the area while considerable consignments of manure came in for the farmers. Much of this came from stables in London with further quantities coming from London Zoo.

145

Potton station in earlier steam days looking towards Gamlingay and Cambridge. The station closed to goods traffic on 1st January 1966 and to passenger traffic on 1st January 1968. (Lens of Sutton)

In December 1914, not long after the outbreak of the First World War, the Bedford to Cambridge line was for a time requisitioned for heavy military traffic. Normal services were suspended while a succession of troop trains covered the line at intervals of 20 minutes. At Cambridge they continued their journey on Great Eastern tracks, enabling a large proportion of Kitchener's Army to eventually reach France. In January 1923 the line became part of the London, Midland & Scottish Railway (LMS) and from 1939, during the Second World War, the line once again saw active service. One role during hostilities was the operation of petrol trains to a RAF supply depot not far from Sandy. Supplies were sent to airfields throughout East Anglia and for the three month period following D-Day over 600 trains left Sandy at the rate of seven a day.

The first suggestion that the line might close came in May 1959 and immediately there was strong local opposition. In the face of this BR introduced new diesel multiple units to encourage traffic and for a time matters improved. In March 1963 the

146

Potton station not long before closure. Happily for posterity the buildings and platforms have been preserved, although as a strictly private residence. (Author)

Beeching Plan was published but it was not until the end of the year that BR announced final closure would be in February 1964. Opposition again proved successful with a suspension obtained pending a public enquiry with the East Anglia & East Midland Transport Users' Consultative Committee. At a meeting held in July 1964 the local authorities strongly pointed out that loss of the service would cause great hardship to the community but BR argued that the line was losing almost £100,000 annually. Despite difficulties in arranging replacement bus services, complete closure came on 1st January 1968 with Bedford St Johns becoming the terminus for trains from Bletchley.

An interesting relic of the former line can be found today at Potton where the station buildings and platforms have survived. On the platform the stanchions with their elegant ironwork continue to support the canopy and the building (now a strictly private residence) carries recollections of the past. Further relics add to the superb realism, even to the small ventilation grilles around the building which carry the letters BCR in script letters.

A further relic from the past is the 0-4-0WT locomotive

147

0-4-0WT Wantage no 5, built 1857, photographed here at the Wantage Tramway. This locomotive at one time served the Sandy & Potton Railway, known as 'Shannon'. (Lens of Sutton)

Shannon. In 1863 this gallant little engine from the Sandy & Potton Railway went to Crewe for 15 years' shunting service, to be sold in 1878 to the Wantage Tramway Company. Following final closure of the tramway in 1945, *Shannon* found numerous further locations and today it stands with pride as a stationary exhibit at the Didcot Railway Centre.

Conclusion

The decline of many branches began in the 1920s. Buses were able to offer a more flexible service than the trains and road haulage was on the increase. In addition the private motor car was beginning to make its presence felt. After nationalisation in 1948, the railways, still recovering from the demands of war service, were slow to meet any competition and were losing ground. Reduced revenue was leading to increased economies and then closures, with the entire pattern of inland transport gradually changing.

An early casualty was the Wolverton & Stony Stratford Tramway which closed in May 1926. Serious competition first came in 1914 when motor buses from Bedford extended their service to Stony Stratford and by the end of the First World War the condition of the trams was described as 'little more than derelict'. The system struggled on, but on 4th May 1926, during the General Strike, services were suspended never to be resumed.

Further closures came when the London Passenger Transport Board decided to discontinue suburban services beyond Aylesbury and in consequence two outposts from the Metropolitan Railway days were closed. The Brill branch (formerly the Wotton Tramway) came to an end on 30th November 1935 and, on 6th July 1936, passenger traffic from Quainton Road to Verney Junction ceased when the line was reduced to single track and used for goods traffic only. The previously-enjoyed building expansion had slowed down and, when the Second World War came, the 'Metro-dream' was at an end.

Another casualty followed soon after the war ended. The 'Nicky Line' from Hemel Hempstead to Harpenden survived the war but passenger services were withdrawn in June 1947 during

149

a coal crisis. Freight struggled on for a time but by the mid-1960s this also ceased. Closures accelerated during the early 1950s as competition increased and the motor car was taking over. Lines that years ago had bustled with traffic such as the Hatfield to St Albans Abbey line or the branches to Aylesbury, Hertford or Rickmansworth all succumbed. In Buckinghamshire, the former GWR branch from Princes Risborough, which crossed the border to Watlington in Oxfordshire, saw its last passenger train in June 1957 after 85 years of faithful service, with closure from 1st July 1957.

In March 1963 proposals were made in a report which became popularly known as the 'Beeching Plan'. Basically the idea was to keep lines considered suitable to rail traffic and give up the remainder. It was claimed that one third of the rail system in Britain carried only 1% of the total traffic! Further drastic cuts inevitably followed and many more lines disappeared. Closures – once a trickle – became a torrent. Where once existed branches, some linking major routes across the region, soon only the original trunk routes remained. A number of isolated branches survived but their future can only be uncertain.

However, the railway's past has not been forgotten. At Quainton Road, steam lives on where one can find a fascinating collection of locomotives and rolling stock. Not only the days of the Metropolitan Railway are recalled but also the time when Sir Edward Watkin had a vision of through trains from the Midlands to the South Coast and beyond to Paris. At Chinnor, it is possible to relive the days of the GWR Princes Risborough to Watlington branch with trains running a 4-mile stretch between Chinnor and Thame Junction. Future plans include the relaying of track to Aston Rowant plus a joint venture with Chiltern Railways to connect with main line traffic through to Marylebone.

Yet what of the future for the Chilterns area? Rail privatisation, we were told, would give us an exciting future. Press reports tell us that 'complaints about late, cancelled and overcrowded trains have soared since the start of rail privatisation. Figures point to an alarming deterioration in services'. The Channel Tunnel, although providing rapid links with European capitals, still has to provide high-speed trains in the UK and the tunnel still has to prove itself financially.

During research in the region, the author was appalled at the very high density of traffic on roads in the Chilterns area, private and commercial. What plans are in hand to avoid total congestion of our highways within just a few years while railway lines remain inadequately used? There is talk, but only talk, of 'piggyback trucks' by rail, a feature popular in many European countries. Container traffic could also surely be maximised. And what is the future for rural train services which remain particularly vulnerable to closure, these alone absorbing a large portion of the railway's annual subsidy?

A brighter aspect of the future is the possibility that light rail might return to redundant lines. The successes of the Docklands Light Railway, the Tyne and Wear Metro and many others have brought about a flood of applications to build new systems elsewhere. There have been numerous proposals over the surviving single track between Luton and Dunstable, one of these being a tramway system giving an eleven-station line to include Luton Airport. On the airport section existing highways would be used. At Milton Keynes, the new town founded in 1967, the council has been considering the possibility of a rapid transit system linking the town centre with Bletchley, Newport Pagnell, Wolverton and Stony Stratford. Where housing near the town centre might make this impractical, then a partially elevated system may be considered. Can we hope for regular passenger services to return between Bicester and Bletchley and that Verney Junction may once again spring back into life?

Is it possible that the former GCR line to Rugby may one day reopen to provide a fast route between the Midlands and the Channel Tunnel? Trains already run again on the restored section between Loughborough Central and Leicester North. And the Buckinghamshire Railway Centre are looking for a link with the Railtrack line with the hope that their trains might run between Quainton Road and Aylesbury and beyond. How Sir Edward Watkin would have been fascinated by such ideas.

Opening and Final Closure Dates of Lines to Regular Passenger Traffic

Line	Opened	Final Closure
Cheddington/Aylesbury	10. 6.1839	2. 2.1953
Dunstable/Leighton Buzzard	1. 6.1848	26. 4.1965
Banbury (Merton Street)/Buckingham	1. 5.1850	2. 1.1961
Buckingham/Verney Junction	1. 5.1850	7. 9.1964
Bletchley/Verney Jct	1. 5.1850	1. 1.1968
Verney Jct/Bicester	1.10.1850	1. 1.1968
Bourne End/High Wycombe	1. 8.1854	2. 5.1970
Hitchin/Bedford	8. 5.1857	1. 1.1962
Sandy/Potton	*1 9.11.1857	1. 1.1968
Hertford/Hatfield	1. 3.1858	18. 6.1951
Luton/Dunstable	3. 5.1858	26. 4.1965
Hatfield/Luton	1. 9.1860	26. 4.1965
Bedford/Sandy/Cambridge	7. 7.1862	1. 1.1968
Princes Risborough/Thame	1. 8.1862	7. 1.1963
Watford/Rickmansworth	1.10.1862	3. 3.1952
St Margarets/Buntingford	3. 7.1863	16.11.1964
Thame/Oxford	24.10.1864	7. 1.1963
Hatfield/St Albans Abbey	16.10.1865	1.10.1951
Wolverton/Newport Pagnell	2. 9.1867	6. 9.1964
Aylesbury/Quainton Road	*2 23. 9.1868	5. 9.1966
Quainton Road/Verney Jct	23. 9.1868	6. 7.1936
Quainton Road/Brill	January 1872	30.11.1935
Bedford/Northampton	10. 6.1872	5. 3.1962
Princes Risborough/Watlington	*3 15. 8.1872	1. 7.1957
Hemel Hempstead/Harpenden	16. 7.1877	16. 6.1947
Wolverton/Stony Stratford	27. 5.1887	4. 5.1926

Quainton Road/Brackley Central/Rugby 15. 3.1899   5. 9.1966
Ashendon jct/Grendon Underwood jct   2. 4.1906   7.12.1953

*1 Merged with Bedford & Cambridge Railway in 1862
*2 Quainton Road has reopened as the Buckinghamshire
   Railway Centre
*3 The section from Chinnor to Thame Junction has reopened as
   the Chinnor & Princes Risborough Railway (the Icknield Line)

Bibliography

In compiling *Lost Railways of the Chilterns*, I have referred to numerous sources, many now out of print, which include the following and which can be recommended for further reading:

Baker, C. *The Metropolitan Railway* (The Oakwood Press)

Cockman, F. G. *The Railways of Hertfordshire* (Hertfordshire Publications)

Cockman, F. G. *Discovering Lost Railways* (Shire Publications Ltd)

Cockman, F. G. *The Railway Age in Bedfordshire* (The Bedfordshire Historical Record Society)

Davies, R. & Grant, M. D. *Forgotten Railways – Chilterns and Cotswolds* (David & Charles)

Edwards, Dennis & Pigram, Ron *The Golden Years of the Metropolitan Railway and the Metroland Dream* (Midas Books)

Goode, C. T. *The Hertford Loop Line* (The Oakwood Press)

Goudie, F. W. & Stuckey, Douglas *West of Watford* (Forge Books)

Joby, R. S. *Forgotten Railways – East Anglia* (David & Charles)

Jones, Ken *The Wotton Tramway (Brill Branch)* (The Oakwood Press)

Leleux, S. A. *The Leighton Buzzard Light Railway* (The Oakwood Press)

Lingard, R. *Princes Risborough – Thame – Oxford Railway* (Oxford Publishing Co)

Paye, P. *The Buntingford Branch* (The Oakwood Press)

Rolt, L. T. C. *Red for Danger* (Pan Books Ltd)

Simpson, Bill *The Banbury to Verney Junction Branch* (Oxford Publishing Co)

Simpson, Bill *Oxford to Cambridge Railway – Volume One: Oxford to Bletchley; Volume Two: Bletchley to Cambridge* (Oxford Publishing Co)

Simpson, Bill *The Aylesbury Railway* (Oxford Publishing Co)

Taylor, Roger, D. & Anderson, Brian *The Hatfield and St Albans Branch of the Great Northern Railway* (The Oakwood Press)

Woodward, G. & S. *The Hatfield, Luton & Dunstable Railway (and on to Leighton Buzzard)* (The Oakwood Press)

INDEX

Winslow 55–56
Winslow Road 38, 39
Wolverton 83–93 *passim*, 151
Wolverton & Stony Stratford
  Tramway 87–93, 149
Wolverton and Stony Stratford and
  District New Tramway Company
  Ltd 90–91

Wooburn Green (formerly Woburn
  Green) 14, 16
Woodford 64
Wood Siding 77
Wotton 67, 68, 74–75, 77
Wotton Tramway 30, 68, 69, 73–82,
  149
Wycombe Railway 11, 14–15, 18, 20